THE SCHOOL MANAGERS

CONTRIBUTIONS IN SOCIOLOGY

Series Editor: Don Martindale
University of Minnesota

CONTRIBUTIONS IN SOCIOLOGY, NUMBER 8

THE
SCHOOL
MANAGERS

POWER AND CONFLICT IN
AMERICAN PUBLIC EDUCATION

*DONALD J. McCARTY
AND CHARLES E. RAMSEY
Foreword by Roald F. Campbell*

GREENWOOD PUBLISHING CORPORATION
WESTPORT, CONNECTICUT

Library of Congress Catalog Card Number: 70-105975
SBN: 8371-3299-1

Greenwood Publishing Corporation
51 Riverside Avenue, Westport, Connecticut 06880

Printed in the United States of America

CONTENTS

v

PART SIX
PROFILES OF POWER AND
RECOMMENDATIONS FOR POLICY

LIST OF TABLES

FOREWORD

This book contributes significantly both to the literature of educational administration and to our knowledge of local government. School managers—board members and superintendents—are viewed in this study in terms of the community context in which they work. Building upon studies of community decision making, the authors posit four community types: dominated, factional, pluralistic, and inert; each one of which tends to be reflected in its school board and in the role the superintendent can play with the board and the community. These conceptions are then examined empirically in fifty-one school districts where each of the four types is represented, and their differentiating characteristics are documented.

Clearly, much that has been said about the training for and the practice of educational administration is called into question by this formulation. Only in pluralistic communities would it appear possible for the superintendent to act consistently as the professional advisor to the board, the ideal set forth in most textbooks. In dominated communities his role seems to be one of caretaker, in factional communities one of political strategist, and in inert communities one of decision-maker. The analysis recognizes that the four types of communities are not always found in pure form; nor does a particular type of community, such as an inert one, always lead to an inert board. Nonetheless, the model posited by the study is generally supported by research findings and does offer a fruitful starting point for thinking about communities and the roles of board members and superintendents in various situations.

Going beyond the mere report of research the authors relate their findings in the fifty-one communities to a wide range of other studies of local government. The discussion is further illuminated by references to current events, employing a frame of reference which provides an explanation for current situations that otherwise appear quite opaque.

If the practice of administration is to be improved by being made more rational and more concerned with humane values—sometimes incompatible objectives—not only must there be better selection of students for administration and more realistic training programs, but communities themselves will have to change. Only when citizens become less tolerant of dominating and inert behavior and develop greater acceptance of a pluralistic society and the need for rational discourse will the roles of boards and superintendents in many of our communities approach our democratic ideal. It is hoped that the relevant insights contained in this book will

come to the attention of citizens, board members, superintendents, administrators in training, and by those who direct
training programs.

ROALD F. CAMPBELL

PREFACE

Throughout history few issues have led to so much misery as the question of who is to control men's destinies. Although it is not in the name of power that armies and mobs have assembled—for it is difficult to rally people around such a symbol—it is power that has been at issue in the battles fought between good kings and bad, kings and feudal lords, over rights and freedoms, over social order versus revolution, and the question of representation in decision-making bodies. The intensity of human passions roused by the problem of power is reflected in the most fundamental and enduring writings of the great thinkers of Western history. For Plato it was a subject of first importance; and the classic controversy between Hobbes and Locke easily translates into the issue of the growth of power and why it is necessary. The later controversy between Marx and Weber is centered on the extent to which power can be seen as the exclusive factor in shaping men's lives. Our intellectual history abounds with still other examples of attempts to define and clarify the nature and functions of power.

During the last two decades, the controversy has continued in sociology, political science, and related areas. No doubt the popular attention this issue has received also grew out of the warning given by President Eisenhower at the end of his term as President against permitting a power elite to develop from among the groups controlling major sectors of our society. President Eisenhower's warning takes on a foreboding significance when it is considered that, objectively, he could be identified with all of the sectors he indicated might join in a single controlling body. The ideas contained in Mills' *The Power Elite* aroused further interest in the structure of power, for in it he hypothesized that such an elite had already actually developed. The public acceptance of the book as at the very least provocative, and at most true—despite diverse critical reactions in intellectual circles —was indicative of the tenor of the period. Concomitant with the growing concern over the existence of a national elite, a parallel controversy has been carried on in the literature of the behavioral sciences over the issue of community power. This controversy, which has also roused public interest, has centered on the issue of whether there does exist an elite group in the community that "calls the shots."

Much of the discussion appears to have been stimulated by a book by Floyd Hunter in which he contends that a study of a large Southern city revealed a controlling power clique that shaped policy and its implementation. Some of these hidden eminences were presumably more powerful than the mayor or the governor, and their responsibility to citizens in general was defined as resting solely upon their view of

themselves as guardians of the basic mores. Such a definition
of responsibility is, of course, unacceptable to our explicit
value system, since there is always the possibility of the in-
trusion of self-interest on the part of any self-appointed
"guardian." This study led to a series of statistical studies
(Hunter's work was based upon content analysis of open-
ended interviews in the main) which either assumed at the
outset or affirmed in conclusion the existence of such a power
elite.

Political scientists, recognizing the implications of such
a hypothesis for their own discipline, immediately set about
their own studies of community power elites. Led by Dahl's
study of a small Northeastern city, political scientists in the
main concluded that such a power elite, if it exists at all,
eludes systematic definition, and even blanketedly denied that
power is structured in the way suggested by Hunter and
others.

The issue remains a question. To begin with, there is a
distressing correlation between differences in findings and
differences in the background of the researcher: sociologists
generally find evidence for an elite structure, while political
scientists uncover another type of structure which might be
described as pluralistic. But even more perplexing is the
methodological issue. The involvement of the intelligent
reading public may inhibit the willingness of behavioral
scientists to expand the point, but different methods do indeed
bring different findings. The different methods used by the
various students of power during the last two decades are
highly correlated with the nature of the conclusions. In general, those who have identified power figures on the basis of
their reputation have been able to identify an elite power

clique controlling the community, while those using less direct but more precise methods have concluded that communities are pluralistic. Critiques of their methodology do not differ basically from the methodological controversies in the past: the open-ended and unstructured methodology of the elite theorists may bring more valid results in intensive case studies, but the data are private and incapable of real replication; while the statistical and structured methods of the pluralists may bring the appearance of precision but the validity of the data is questionably naive and superficial.

The work reported in the pages to follow is an attempt to resolve the issue of elite versus pluralistic structures, and to answer various other critiques regarding the theory of power structure. This attempt involves two thrusts: (a) a typology of power structures which posits both elite and pluralistic structures, and others as well, and (b) the report of the study of fifty-one communities in the Midwest and the Northeast in which this typology was tested. Broadly speaking our thesis is that there are both elite and pluralistic, as well as other types of community structure which are defined and described in the pages to follow. We also posit that for a more complete theory of power it is necessary to indicate over whom that power is exercised. We contend that if there is community-wide power then it is exercised over community-wide boards and through these boards over professional employees in the institutional orders of the community. We further contend that the way in which decision-making is structured in these boards and the way the professionals play their roles varies with the type of community power structure.

Because of the numerous difficulties in any study of

power, and especially in an extensive study of several communities rather than an intensive study of one, we chose to limit ourselves to one institutional order, namely, education. Such a selection can be justified on several grounds other than the purely practical limitation mentioned. The fundamental character of our society is as much influenced by the knowledge explosion as by any other trend. It can be argued that the civil rights issue, the pollution issue, the poverty issue, and the war have become the focus of attention as much due to the increased information relating to them as to the problems themselves. After all, these problems have been with us for a long time without much public attention being paid them. Furthermore, vast social resources in money, time, and effort, in the defense department, the space agency, HEW, and in the private sector, clearly are directed towards magnifying this explosion of information. Since the school is a center of the knowledge explosion, it might be thought that in the decades to come, what is being done now in the schools will to a great extent shape our future.

A more mundane justification centers around the school as big business in almost any community—whether that size is based upon the number of people directly involved or the budget. Therefore, if power is operating anywhere, it is important to understand the significance it might have in the educational institution. If power does indeed exist outside the formal channels of elected and appointed officials, then in a relatively open society we must recognize that any general policies approved by the public, either directly or indirectly through its representatives, will be greatly affected by how those exercising such power view these policies.

In reporting the results of this study in the context of

the typology or model suggested by the present authors, we begin by attempting to summarize the literature in terms of the substantive problems found. Chapter 1 is a summary of this literature organized around the substantive issues, and the presentation of our typology. In Part Two we describe the dynamics and perception of power in communities classified as dominated, a classification consistent with studies on the "elite" model. This description is extended to decision-making by the school board and to the way in which superintendents perceive their role and are perceived by others. In Part Three we attempt to describe the dynamics of decision-making in communities which we call factional, meaning simply that these communities are characterized by conflict between two or three large factions. Again attention is focused not only on the community itself, but on the school and the superintendent. In Part Three we turn our attention to those many communities which fit the pluralistic model. In Part Four we report the dynamics of decision-making in communities where no power structure was found operating behind the school board and superintendent. Here, attention is upon the role of the superintendent, since in these communities he is indeed the decision-maker. In Part Five the findings for the fifty-one communities are summarized in a more statistical rhetoric with suggestions for future research and policy making. In the Appendix we discuss again the literature on power, this time centered around methodological problems, and report the methods used in the present study.

The authors developed the typology around which these research findings are organized in the school year 1960–61 when both were professors at Cornell University. The typology was a further development of an initial step in this direction by McCarty.[1] The empirical study reported in this book was co-sponsored by the United States Office of Education, project no. 2891, and the Agricultural Experiment Station at the University of Minnesota. The points of view or opinions stated, do not necessarily represent the position or policy of either agency.

In the decade during which our project developed from a model to an empirical study to the long delayed final reports, we have become indebted to many people. Above all, we owe those influential persons, the superintendents and the much harried school board members, a sincere thank you for suffering through our persistent scrutiny. Having promised to keep their trust confidential, we cannot name them, but without their cooperation this study would not have been possible.

1689

Our field interviewers, John Comstock, Joseph Di Stefano, Michael Gonta, Rose Hanson, Eugene Karies, Lou Kutcher, Mark Shibles, Alec Warren, Bill Wilson, and Joseph Zizzi performed yeoman service. Interviewing in the field requires limitless energy and quick intelligence. These conscientious colleagues fully met these rigorous criteria and we are grateful to them for their superlative contributions.

Stanley Wells Pollack, field chief in the Midwest, deserves particular mention. He contributed in several capacities, including assisting on the research design, helping us work out difficulties in field operations, and consulting on myriad other issues. Edward Hickcox, field chief in the East,

---

1. Donald J. McCarty, "Motives For Seeking School Board Membership" (Unpublished Ph.D. dissertation, Dept. of Education, University of Chicago, 1959).

likewise performed commendably in a host of key assignments, and along with Joseph Di Stefano and Mark Shibles gave us the benefit of his critical comments. David Klemmack's assistance in the statistical analysis was indispensable.

Mary J. Husting superintended the completion of this manuscript through many phases with remarkably good cheer, persistence, and understanding. Jeannette Morgan and Mary Lou Jorissen gave unstintingly of their time in preparing the manuscript.

C.E.R.

D.J.M.

PART ONE

THE PROBLEM
OF POWER

The most problematic aspect in the study of power is determining its structure, not whether it actually exists. The sum of written works on power at the community level indicates that it is either pluralistic or that an elite group calls on lower echelons to carry out certain policies. In the first chapter we discuss this problem in the light of the current literature and suggest that there are pluralistic communities and communities dominated by an elite. We further see two other types of communities, those fraught with intense conflict between two or three large factions and those in which power is inert, although potentially there. Another important question regarding power is over whom it is exercised. We suggest that within the community it is exercised over community-wide boards and professional workers.

Our suggestions take the form of a model consisting of (a) various structures of community power, (b) various structures of decision-making on community-wide boards, and (c) various types of roles played by the professional workers in the community. The central notion of the model is that the structures and roles are interrelated—the nature of the power structure affects the nature of decision-making, which in turn affects the way a professional must play his role if he is to survive in that community.

1

THE MODEL
OF POWER
AND CONFLICT

The man on the street will hardly question whether power exists in his community, for he experiences it daily in earning a living, in his leisure activities, and in rearing his children. Sociologists, educators and political scientists will likewise agree that power relations are present in their own work situations, their families, and in many of the contacts they have with agencies and institutional orders in their communities.

Words like power, authority, influence, dominance, coercion, and persuasion have had a long-standing usage in the English language, and for centuries have been effective in communicating the idea that at some times, some persons or groups must submit to the will of other persons or groups, regardless of personal wishes and generally accepted values. Even our slang expressions have incorporated a jargon that communicates the existence of power in a most denotative manner: "he calls the shots," "he tells me what to do and I do it," "he's a big wig," "he's a VIP," "he is in the driver's seat," "I'm a nobody." In its empirical state, then, the existence of power is not at issue.

The controversy over the nature of power that has raged during the last two decades in the works of sociologists, political scientists, and scholars in related fields is comparable in intensity to any major theoretical dispute in the recent history of the behavioral sciences. Not content to discuss concepts in all cases, critics have hinted that some theorists and researchers have been overzealous in their attempts to advance a particular hypothesis.

Much of the debate has centered on the issue of whether power relations in a community represent an "elite" model or a "pluralistic" one. In the elite model the decisions on important policy matters are made by a man or a few men, usually not those officially assigned that decision-making responsibility by virtue of their office.[1] In the pluralistic model, power is both situational and temporary, and even the participation of persons in the decision-making process is not predictable from one situation to another.[2]

The differences of opinion found in the literature are due to many factors. The problem itself has too often been posed in either-or terms. The dependence upon case studies of single communities accounts in some measure for the lack of agreement among researchers, and differences in methods have led to differences in results. Nonetheless, we suggest, different findings may occur because there are, indeed, different kinds of power structures.

The controversy is a reflection of the state of our theories and ways of conceptualizing power. Some conceptual issues were important in the design and conduct of the present study and a brief summary of these is presented in the following paragraphs. No attempt is made to be exhaustive, either to the implications of all the conceptual problems or to the literature bearing upon them.

PROBLEMS IN THE THEORY OF POWER

Definitions of power differ and the correspondence between definitions and empirical descriptions found in research studies is often problematic. Most disconcerting of all, contradictions are found between studies which apparently have been done with equal care.

The classic definition, cited at some time by almost every student of power, is that of Max Weber who, writing before World War I, defined power in a way which set the pattern for most later definitions: "In general, we understand by power the chance of a man or of a number of men to realize their own will in a communal action even against the resistance of others who are participating in the action." [3] The word "chance" may mean "empirical probability," but such an interpretation is not always clearly assigned. For example, Rose says of this definition:

> His use of the word "chance" implies that Weber considered the actual realization of one's will rather incidental to the basic problem of power. To be sure, one must "have a chance" in order to realize one's will, but the two con-

cepts are by no means identical. . . . Much of the contemporary literature has substituted "ability" or "potential"
for Weber's "chance," but maintains the distinction between this potential, and actual realization of will.[4]

Rose goes on to cite students of power who see power
as potential, although in these definitions it is possible that
the writers would see the *evidence* of the potential in the
actual exercise of power:

> 1. Power will denote the capacity or potential of persons
> in certain statuses to set conditions, make decisions, and/
> or take actions which are determinative for the existence
> of others within a given social system.[5]

> 2. The term "power" refers to the ability or authority of
> individuals or organizations to control, effectively guide,
> or influence other individuals or groups.[6]

> 3. Power in its most general sense refers to a capacity or
> ability to control others and . . . to control the decision-
> making process.[7]

Especially important in interpreting the words of this last
definition in terms of the problem of actual versus potential
power is the further statement by these authors: "Persons
who exercise power must, by definition, have had a power
potential, but not all persons who hold potential power do in
fact exercise power."[8] The distinction between actual and potential power is important in the theory of power and excellent
discussions from different points of view are given in D'Antonio
and Form,[9] Dahl,[10] and Polsby.[11]

The distinction between actual and potential power is
also an important one for empirical research. The concept
of potential power greatly lessens the obligation of the researcher to demonstrate that power figures actually bring

about decisions, even against the wishes of others. It is evident in some studies that such a concept leads to amassing evidence to indicate the possession of resources for power with little demonstration of the effective use of those resources in actual decision-making. Such research reports often leave the impression that it requires vast resources to accomplish even comparatively little in actual results.

A second unresolved difficulty in the theory concerns the degree to which power stems from the activities of those who wield it or from those subject to it. The common sense notion of power involves forceful figures demanding and commanding. In most cases where power originates with power figures, the "velvet glove" is more nearly consistent with the dynamics of power. The typical power figure does not yell or even command, and he certainly does not pound the desk. Typically, he is a gentleman of grace and poise. He has the "bait" and knows how to hold out that bait without explicitly offering rewards in return for cooperation and conformity. Indeed, such a concept seems permissible even in those theories which rely on the self-interest model or on that in modern terminology called exchange theory. The controller and the controlled exchange, respectively, control for favors, but both are tempered by the amount of emotional involvement and investment each has in the outcome.[12]

Even more typically, we find power relations originating with the controlled—those who would ingratiate themselves by asking for guidance. Naturally, those who are asked for guidance are those who control valued resources—money and employment especially but not exclusively. We find in some communities that there are persons who are sought out, and because it is known that they are sought out, others seek them out. The power this reputation gives the person may not be due to his initiation. The problem of who initiates power relations depends in part on the problem of "levels" or "types" of power.

Levels of power and differences in its qualitative manifestation have been recognized in many conceptual schemes although the word "power" is usually reserved for the more deliberate and direct attempts to control on the part of the powerful. Two clear conceptualizations which include the fundamental distinctions are the following offered by Martindale and Biertstedt:

> 1. Influence means that ideas or a plan of action sponsored by some men are followed by others in preference to alternatives. The extent to which this is true is the measure of influence of the first over the second. Every group and every community presents a pattern (or more usually, patterns) of influence. Such influence may be informal or formal; it may be persuasive or coercive. When influence is coercive, backed up and maintained by physical sanctions, it may be described as social power. The relation between influence and social power can be formulated in one of two ways: Influence may be defined as the general category of behavior including both coercive and non-coercive persuasion; social power may be described as coercive influence." [13]

> 2. For reasons which possess considerable cogency, it seems desirable also to maintain a distinction between influence and power. The most important reason perhaps is that influence is persuasive while power is coercive. We submit voluntarily to influence but power requires submission. [14]

Although the above distinction appears to be necessary, we found it less clear than we would have liked for research purposes. Bell also finds the distinction less than clear, and in criticizing Mills he says:

> It is quite true that violence, as Weber has said, is the ultimate sanction of power, and in extreme situations control of the means of violence may be decisive in seizing or holding power. But neither is power the inexorable, implacable, granitic force that Mills and others make it to be. . . . Power in Mills' terms is domination. But we do not need an elaborate discussion to see that this view of power avoids more problems than it answers—particularly once one moves away from the outer boundary of power as violence to institutionalized power, with which Mills is concerned. For in society . . . where violence is not the rule, we are in the realm of norms, values, traditions, legitimacy, consensus, leadership, and identification—all the modes and mechanisms of command and authority, their acceptance or denial, which shape action in the day-to-day world without violence." [15]

In our study we find that certain persons and groups consistently are able to embody these values, norms, and traditions. Such consistent control, though accomplished through the more subtle psychological process of identifying certain persons as best expressing values and interests, is best regarded as part of the power structure, so long as the control is a process of clearly demonstrable interaction.

The distinction between power and influence is useful, but we believe further refinements will be necessary to adequately describe the power relations within the community (using "power" as a generic term). One such set of refinements is that suggested by Schermerhorn: [16]

> under pressure [in a relationship] there is effort and constraint. Five subforms of this pressure relationship may be

listed: (1) submission to a leader or a dominant figure who embodies informal group norms; (2) submission to a leader who is an expert, who has rational qualifications; (3) submission to a leader in view of his office, that is, to an institutional figure; (4) submission to a person because of his strength or superior ability to use violence; and (5) submission to a dominant figure as a matter of habit.

This listing assumes that in an important way, power generates from the controlled.

Many authors have pointed to the importance of specifying the person(s) or group(s) over whom control is exercised. If power is conceived of as a social relation, then the powerful must control some person or group in the social structure. This concept is present in Weber's previously cited definition, in the phrase "even against the resistance of others who are participating in the action." On this point, Emerson says:

> The underdeveloped state of this area is further suggested by what appears, to this author, to be a recurrent flaw in common conceptions of social power; a flaw which helps to block adequate theoretical development as well as meaningful research. That flaw is the implicit treatment of power as though it were an attribute of a person or group (X is an influential person, Y is a powerful group). Given this conception, the natural research question becomes, 'Who in community X are the power holders?' . . . To say that X has power is vacant unless we specify over whom.[17]

Emerson further states that "in making these necessary qualifications, we force ourselves to face up to the obvious: power is a property of the social relation; it is not an attribute of the actor." [18]

If we are to fully understand how power is structured, it is necessary to look still further for an explanation. We contend that within the same system there is a very wide variety of relationships which must be understood before it is possible to describe the power structure accurately.

The existence of the seeds of conflict in power relations is implicit in definitions which contain statements, as Weber's does, such as "even against the will of others." Can power exist without the conflict of wills in this definition? We believe that it can and does, but an "acid" test of whether power exists might best be made when disagreement does exist.

The two-way relationship between the development of theory and the refinement of research demands that the researcher proceed with the best concepts available, hoping that his research will allow for the improvement of these concepts in later formulations.

THE OPERATIONAL DEFINITION OF POWER

The researcher must have some operational definition of variables, usually derived from concepts used in the theoretical formulations in the field. The difficulties encountered in deriving operational definitions from theoretical concepts were indicated in the foregoing paragraphs, but these difficulties simply delineate problems and do not excuse us from attempts at construct validity.

In the present work, social power is operationally de-

fined to include three necessary elements. The first occurs
when a person or group is reported, in specific instances, to
have realized their will, usually against what we might reasonably assume to be someone else's wishes. We have, throughout, *preferred* to classify community power relations on the
basis of those instances where both the controlled and those
controlling give similar reports of the circumstances. We do
not wish to ignore the concept of "potential power," but in
the classification of communities and in the description of
the dynamics of power and conflict, we lean wherever possible on the experiences reported by those directly involved.
In this way, we believe we have avoided "rumor" completely,
although we have not avoided the perceptual nature of our
data nor of our conclusions. We depend upon informants:
informants who have experienced power relations and conflict, and who report their perceptions of self-other relations.
From these perceptions we infer our own classifications and
dynamics, an unavoidable step in all research, but all the
more obvious when the raw data which we perceive are
themselves perceptions.

A second necessary element of social power in our
working definition is that we must specify who is controlled,
as well as who is doing the controlling. We construct a model
of these relationships, indicating that, in general, the community controls the community-wide board or committee, and
that board in turn controls the professional. But in this model
there are two reservations. First, we limit ourselves primarily
to educational policy making, thereby legitimatizing certain
power relationships in the directions indicated by the model.
Second, by specifying who is controlling (influencing) and
who is controlled (influenced) we place power and conflict

in the context of a relationship rather than positing them as attributes of a person or group, thus eliminating the mechanistic nature of the relationships posited by the model.

The third element of the working definition of social power is the specification of some type of interaction between the controlled and the controlling groups. That is, the simple probability of a group achieving its wishes may come not from power at all, unless power is broadly defined to include the ability to manipulate any resources. In a way, a person who moves from the inner city to a suburb has increased his power over his family's life chances, since suburban schools are usually more effective in achieving the aims of middle-class America. However, this is hardly the kind of power relation that is central to the theory of power. Rather, the interaction between leaders and followers lies at the heart of our observations. This interaction need not be direct, for conformity may be channeled through an extremely complicated social structure. If a body of decision-makers wishes to instigate a certain policy, it is hardly necessary for them to be in direct contact with all of the individual citizens or the children in the school for this power to be interactive; the interaction is through the channels of organization.

This definition does not preclude most of the generalizations which the various researchers, theorists, and critics have discussed in the literature on power. Indeed, the definition permits inclusion under the rubric of power such diverse types of relationships as legitimate and illegitimate power, coercion and influence, power through personal charisma and that through group organization, and, as will be seen, domination, conflict, and pluralism.

The main concern of those in the controversy over power

is not the existence of power but its structure. That individual A controls individual B at certain times in certain situations is denied by no one. However, when we begin to see a repetitive pattern of individual A controlling individual B, and relate this further to the way in which each relates to individual C, we are approaching the central concept of social structure, or power structure. It would be useful to review this concept to establish the guidelines of the analysis to follow.

By structure is meant a "relatively fixed relationship between elements, parts, or entities." [19] In the social structure, these fixed relationships exist for varying degrees of time and may be found to exist between individuals, between an individual and a group, between groups, or between other relevant units. There is no reason why groups or individuals must be the unit of analysis in all sociological work. Books, ideas, buildings, rituals, and documents may all be related to each other or to individuals or groups, and seen as part of a social structure. Where the recurrent patterns of human behavior and human relationships exist, it is the job of the social scientist to describe and explain. Furthermore, there is nothing in the concept of structure, *per se,* that implies that the observation of structure is easy or difficult. Structural relationships may be so apparent as to be obvious to the man on the street or they may be so hidden as to evade the grasp of social scientists with all of the tools of observation they possess. The complex power structure of contemporary society is of an evasive, difficult character. The vast array of empirical power relations discernible in the present-day community suggests that there is much work to be done to accurately portray the structural types and components which will explain, predict, and eventually control individual events. That is to say, we must see how one type of power relationship affects another and is affected by it; how authority based on formal office relates to personal dominance, interpersonal conflict and the like.

The central focus of the analysis to follow is on the problem of how power, seen in individual and empirical events, can be viewed as a power structure. How does such a structure develop, and how does it operate dynamically? What are the various types of relationships which may develop between the community, the community-wide board, and the role of the professional?

We hypothesize that the structure of relations within the community provides the background which both limits and facilitates certain kinds of actions in legally constituted boards and committees and in the professional roles of people in that community. We do not suggest that the community power structure is the only influence in the community having an effect on boards and professional roles, but to the extent that there is some freedom of interpretation allowed the board and the professional, the informal power structure may have a considerable amount to say about how that interpretation is to be made.

THE MODEL

Critics of researchers and theorists who have maintained the existence of a "power elite" have questioned, on the basis of their studies, whether such an elite in fact exists. They claim that communities are actually pluralistic in structure and belief. While the research methods of elitists and pluralists have differed, we believe that their differences in findings are not entirely the result of methodological differences. Most of the studies seem carefully done, given the limitations of methodology in new fields of investigation.

We feel, rather, that the conclusions represent differences in substantive findings. One of the main theses of the present work is that *power varies from one community to another in patterns capable of description.*

A second criticism of power theories is that often it is not stated over whom power is held. If we begin by identifying power figures in a community, we must also identify those over whom these power figures exercise control. A second thesis of this work is that *community power is held over members of community-wide boards and over professionals implementing the policies of those boards.*

Some theorists, and we concur, point to the fact that sociology is concerned with social interaction or social relationships, and therefore power is best viewed as a relationship—in other words, as part of a structure. A third thesis of this work is that *the power relationship is seen most directly through the interaction and relationships between community power figures, community-wide boards, and professionals, with these relationships constituting a power structure.*

The fourth thesis of this work is that *the power structure, composed of these interrelationships, itself varies, and that this variation forms various patterns some of which allow people to adjust to and predict the situation, and others which do not.*

Although the model presented below is specifically addressed to school systems, we believe it is also applicable to other systems where boards, committees, and professionals are dependent upon more inclusive social systems.

Types of Communities

The "elite power model" we shall call the *dominated power structure*. This concept holds that the power structure in a community is pyramidal with a few men or one man at the top. The decisive decision-making group is likely to be the economic elite of the community. Although dominance in various situations may also derive from religion, ethnicity, political party, race, or whatever, in matters of "big policy" the power structure directs the course of events in the community. "Big policy" includes educational matters. The key point is that opposition viewpoints to the policies advocated by the dominant group toward school affairs do not appreciably influence the behavior of the board or the superintendent. This model of power has been criticized as biased by those who consider stratification analysis outmoded, but it may be accepted that at least some communities follow this pattern in leadership relations. Important for the present study design, however, is the possibility of the existence of other types of power structures.

The elite power model does not provide for conflict between sides of relatively even strength. Yet, there are some communities in which at least two durable factions compete for control over important decisions. In these situations are found not only relatively even sides but also clear manifestations of power within each faction similar to those in the single elite power model. These factors tend to coalesce around natural rallying points such as religion, politics, occupation (as in town versus gown), and economic philosophy. This type we shall call the *factional power structure*.

There are considerable data suggesting that some communities follow neither the elite nor the factional power model. Rather, the power structure is pluralistic or diffused, with many poles of power. Theoretically, there is no single a priori power structure which must be reckoned with in any situation. This we shall call the *pluralistic power structure*. Power and community interests exist, but power is contestable. The dispersion of power, or the lack of domination, does not, however, mean that the schools operate in a laissez-faire manner. On the contrary, there is likely to be high interest in education since people from various strata of the community may be very active in school affairs.

A fourth type of power structure is frequently seen in small rural communities although it may exist elsewhere. This residual type of community reveals no active power structure. Power is basically inert, or, more properly, latent, and resembles a sort of domination by the status quo. Selection of board members, for instance, is likely to be done by finding someone willing to take the job regardless of his qualifications, interests, or viewpoints. In such an environment radical experimentation is not likely to occur. We shall call this type the *inert power structure*.

Types of Boards

Boards of education do exhibit a type of decision-making that corresponds to the particular kind of community power structure of which they are a part. The dominated power structure results in a *dominated board*. Board members ⸜ chosen on the assumption that since they share the ideology of the dominant group, they will take the advice of community leaders. Economic control over the board members by community influentials often strengthens their control. In such a situation, a majority board, or perhaps one or two powerful individuals, represents the community elite and exercises power so that policy follows the desired direction. Members of dominated boards are not necessarily consciously aware of the impact of homogeneity on board decision-making. By definition, there is no organized opposition of any magnitude contesting for office.

In the community with a factional power structure, a *factional school board* is found. Voting is more important than discussion at board meetings; if the vote is crucial the majority faction always wins. Board members represent the viewpoint of one or the other of the factions and tend to act according to the ideology of the group they represent. Board elections are hotly contested. One particular faction may be in control of the board at any one time, but the balance is likely to shift as new members are selected.

In the community with a pluralistic power structure, school board members may often represent particular interests, but there is no overall theme of power influence. Therefore, it is in this type of community that school board members will be active but not rigidly bound to one position. Discussion, often before a motion, is of utmost importance. Board members are equal in status and treat each other as colleagues free to act as individuals. We shall call this type of board the *status congruent school board*. Rather than a hierarchy of control within the board, there exists a com-

munity of peers whose decisions are characterized by full
discussion of problems and arrival at consensus in an atmosphere of detachment from the interests of any particular
segment of the community.

In the community with the inert power structure, the
school board is inactive and has no philosophical reinforcement from the community. It tends to perform perfunctorily
because board members neither represent nor receive reinforcement from citizens for expressing one viewpoint or another. When decisions have to be made, the board tends to
follow the lead of the professional staff without going exten-
sively into the appropriateness of a policy in terms of community needs or desires. It simply sanctions policies
presented to it. It is a *sanctioning board* which does little
but exercise its right to approve or reject proposals from the
community or the administration.

Roles of the Professional

Now let us relate this conceptual model to the behavior of
superintendents. There are certain patterns of activity which,
logically, the superintendent must exhibit in each case, and
which may be generalized in the analytical sense.

In the dominated community and board, the superintendent must play the role of *functionary* if he is to act
effectively as the integrator of community interests and
school programs. He tends to identify with the dominant
interests and takes his cues for action from them. Needless
to say, he may do this as a matter of conscience, since he is
probably in complete agreement with proposals offered by
the elitist group. He perceives himself as an administrator

who carries out policy rather than as a developer of policy. The school board, either unconsciously or deliberately, will choose a superintendent who holds beliefs and follows behavior patterns consistent with prevailing themes in the dominated community. So long as this person agrees with the dominant ideology, all necessary business will continue to be done in his office, but he will not be a true decision-maker.

In the factional community and board, the superintendent must work with the majority, and, since these communities often change majorities, he must be careful not to become too closely identified with one faction. In other words, he must be a *political strategist.* He takes his direction from the faction exercising power at any particular time, but he behaves in such a way that he can also work effectively with the opposing group when the power balance shifts. Rather than taking a strong stand on controversial issues, he takes a middle course, allowing himself room for retreat.

In the community with a pluralistic power structure and status congruent board, the superintendent is expected to give professional advice based on the best educational research and theory. The board is active but open-minded. He is a *professional advisor.* He is not limited to carrying out policy handed down to him, nor is he forced to shape his opinions according to the ideology of the group in power. His approach can be more statesmanlike in the sense that he can express to the board alternative policies, and he can delineate the consequences of any action openly and objectively.

In the community with the inert power structure and the sanctioning board, the superintendent initiates action and the board acts merely as a rubber stamp. In this case the role of the superintendent is that of *decision-maker*. He does not have to take cues from any dominant group nor is he called on to give technical advice as a basis for decision. Because of the lack of interest on the part of the board, the superintendent not only is free to initiate action in substantive matters, but must do so if the program is to be effective.

The preceding descriptive account of community power structure and school administration may be summarized as follows:

TYPES OF COMMUNITY POWER

COMMUNITY POWER STRUCTURE	SCHOOL BOARD	ROLE OF THE SUPERINTENDENT
Dominated	Dominated	Functionary
Factional	Factional	Political strategist
Pluralistic	Status congruent	Professional adviser
Inert	Sanctioning	Decision-maker

In the pages to follow, we attempt to describe the sources and dynamics of these various types of power relations. The descriptions are based upon interviews taken with fifty-one school superintendents, the school board members in those fifty-one school districts, and community leaders and power figures in each of those school districts. The description of the methodology employed is presented in Appendix A.

NOTES

1. Robert S. Lynd and Helen M. Lynd, *Middletown in Transition*, New York: Harcourt, Brace and Co., 1937. Floyd Hunter, *Community Power Structure*, Chapel Hill: University of North Carolina Press, 1953. William V. D'Antonio and Eugene C. Erickson, "The Reputational Technique as a Measure of Community Power: An Evaluation Based on Comparative and Longitudinal Studies, *American Sociological Review*, 27, June, 1962, pp. 363–376, and others.

2. Robert A. Dahl, *Who Governs?* New Haven: Yale University Press, 1961. Robert A. Dahl, *Modern Political Analysis,* Englewood Cliffs: Prentice-Hall, Inc., 1965. Nelson W. Polsby, *Community Power and Political Theory,* New Haven: Yale University Press, 1963. Raymond E. Wolfinger, "Reputation and Reality in the Study of 'Community Power'," *American Sociological Review,* 25, October, 1960, pp. 636–644, and others.

3. Max Weber, *From Max Weber: Essays in Sociology,* H. H. Gerth and C. W. Mills, eds., New York: Oxford University Press, 1946, p. 180.

4. Arnold Rose, *The Power Structure: Political Process in American Society,* New York: Oxford University Press, 1967, pp. 45–46.

5. Robert O. Schulze, "The Bifurcation of Power in a Satellite City," in Morris Janowitz, ed., *Community Political Systems,* Glencoe, Illinois: The Free Press, 1961, p. 259.

6. John L. Haer, "Social Stratification in Relation to Attitude Toward Sources of Power in a Community," *Social Forces,* 35, December, 1956, p. 137.

7. William V. D'Antonio and Howard J. Ehrlich, eds.,

Power and Democracy in America, Notre Dame, Indiana: University of Notre Dame Press, 1961, p. 132.

8. Ibid., p. 132.

9. William V. D'Antonio and William H. Form, *Influentials in Two Border Cities: A Study in Community Decision-Making,* Notre Dame, Indiana: University of Notre Dame Press, 1965.

10. Robert A. Dahl, *Who Governs?*

11. Polsby, *Community Power and Political Theory.*

12. Richard M. Emerson, "Power-Dependence Relations," *American Sociological Review,* 17, February, 1962, pp. 31–41.

13. Don Martindale, *Institutions, Organizations, and Mass Society,* Boston: Houghton Mifflin Company, 1966, p. 292.

14. Robert M. Bierstedt, "An Analysis of Social Power," *American Socioligical Review,* 15, 1950, p. 731.

15. Daniel Bell, *The End of Ideology,* Glencoe: The Free Press, 1962, p. 52.

16. Richard A. Schermerhorn, *Society and Power,* New York: Random House, 1964, p. 6.

17. Emerson, "Power Dependence Relations," p. 31.

18. Ibid.

19. Robin M. Williams, *American Society,* New York: Alfred A. Knopf, 1967, p. 20.

PART TWO

THE DOMINATED COMMUNITY, THE DOMINATED BOARD, AND THE SUPERINTENDENT AS FUNCTIONARY

In the dominated community there is clear-cut evidence that special groups exercise considerable control over the policies of the school board and over the way in which the superintendent plays his role. Although no attempt was made in the present study to analyze types of motivation leading to submission to dominant powers, there are instances throughout these data which transverse the range from voluntary submission to control to cases of outright coercion.

The criteria we preferred for classifying a board as dominated was the admission of the controlled to being controlled, rather than the statement of dominant figures that they did the controlling, although we would like both to report the same event. It is possible for those in control to feel they have more power than they actually have, or, in a highly dominated community, to disavow their dominance.

The superintendent's role in a dominated community must be that of functionary; he implements policy, services the organization, anticipates trouble and quells it when it arises.

2

CONSENSUS
AND CONTROL

In our sample the burden of proof for whether a community was dominated lay with those who experienced it as such. Consequently, there were probably more dominated communities in the sample than were so classified. However, we wished to avoid the criticism often levelled at theorists and researchers who have studied dominated patterns, that power had not actually been effectively demonstrated.

One city included in the study had a population of approximately 35,000 and was about average or somewhat above in income and level of living. Persons living "on the hill" had quite high incomes, though there were few who were wealthy. Families living in "the flats" had relatively low incomes, but there was no extreme poverty. Provisions for a technical education, the type often thought of as most appropriate for low-income children, had been largely neglected in favor of a stiff college preparatory curriculum.

The school system consistently ranked among the highest in the state in national merit scholars.

An honest effort was made to get a Negro on the school board at each election, but the one Negro who had served by far the longest term and was best qualified, was a well-known surgeon in the region and too burdened by other duties to continue his tenure. In fact, his reputation was so substantial that he was consulted in more cases of surgery than any other physician in town. Although he had an opportunity to develop a white clientele among the upper middle class because of his knowledge and skill, he preferred to work with the poor down on the flats.

At one point this physician decided that he would not be able to run for the school board any more. The nominating committee for the school board found that it could not "find leadership" among the poor in the flats, since it could not find a candidate who would not upset the normal operations of the school board. The committee finally settled upon a quiet businessman whose customers were primarily minority group members but who himself was white. He was neither highly respected nor looked down upon by the minority group members, and in discussions with a few of the minority group members we discovered that he was not considered to be their representative.

The school board was made up of seven members, and the decision-making process ran smoothly. Aside from the representative from the flats, the board was composed of two college professors, a real estate man, a businessman, and two women who participated in community affairs. We could not determine that any of these people were high in the power structure, but neither were they regarded as potential troublemakers.

There was a latent aggregate of social conditions which could lead to factionalism in the community. Labor unions were not strong, but there was a reasonably heavy Catholic electorate, and also a medium-sized college in town. Although the elections for mayor and city council swung back and forth between Democratic and Republican, the labor-management issue, the town and gown split, and the evenness of the two-party split did not result in conflict. In general, the professors were heavily committed to their research programs, the Republicans and Democrats cooperated, and the Catholics and labor unions were relatively inert.

The superintendent was a person who had published research and other articles on education, and gave the appearance of being a true decision-maker. At board meetings he told the board members the professional criteria for decisions and framed his recommendations along the lines of self-interest. Since the board members were interested in good schools and respectful of professional criteria, they did not oppose him. In general, the community power figures assumed the school system was in good hands and they had ceased careful monitoring of school elections. One telling event showed, however, how the domination of the community could come into play at any given time.

The event was sparked by two of the less satisfied board members joining two persons who were dissatisfied with the superintendent's method of operation. Like his predecessor, who had enjoyed long tenure and a distinguished reputation, the superintendent had grown accustomed to running the schools as he saw fit. Since he was in the power structure at a fairly low echelon he felt secure.

It is significant that the members of the board who began to question the superintendent's tactics had been selected by a community-wide caucus; they had not campaigned against the superintendent's policies and practices. In fact, their quiet personal nature led many people to believe— especially the community leaders—that these persons would act reasonably, dependably and tractably. Nor did the group who began the criticism represent a single faction: two were professors, each with a different philosophy of education, and the third, who had been on the board for some time, held a personal grudge against the superintendent's wife. Prior to the arrival of the superintendent this board member had been the organist in the most prestigious church in the city, but the superintendent's wife, also an accomplished organist, had then assumed this task. The fourth member of the board was a businessman who ran a small store and was financially independent of the major banks.

These four persons met before the first board meeting of the year, and decided to fire the superintendent on the grounds that he was neglecting the school system and was more interested in publication and in "big time operations" in the community.

At the first board meeting, the superintendent was taken completely by surprise when he was told that he should seek another job. Although his contract was not terminated, he was warned that it would be. This gave him the opportunity to resign voluntarily, at least in appearance, since the members of the board who were against him were not anxious for a fight within the community.

At this point, the superintendent did not wholly believe that the board members were sincere in their threat, or that they could implement the statement made to him. He therefore did very little to seek employment elsewhere; nor, strangely enough, did he consult his powerful backers in the community.

At the second board meeting, asked if he had made a search for new employment, he said that he had not, and the board told him that he was fired. The vote was four to three, with the four members briefly described voting to fire him. Completely taken aback, he was unprepared to retaliate at that moment.

After the firing, the superintendent called the vice-president of one of the two largest banks in town and the general manager of the most prominent industry, a subsidiary of a large national corporation. He told them he had been fired, and they too were surprised at the action. These two then arranged a meeting to discuss what to do. The superintendent had been a good public servant in their opinion. He had run an effective school district and kept taxes low by taking advantage of graduate student wives as teachers in the school system. The company manager got in touch with the presidents of the other two large banks in town, the newspaper editor, who was higher in the power structure than is ordinarily found, and a lawyer whose power came not from his law practice but from the fact that he was a member of a once wealthy and highly prestigious family in the community.

Having met, the group discussed whether or not to back the superintendent. They decided to leave it up to the superintendent and to have another meeting and talk to him. This first meeting, as well as the second meeting, took place in the bank of the vice-president whom the superintendent first called.

At the second meeting the superintendent made his third mistake, the first having been his attempt to play the role of a political strategist when actually he was a servant of the power structure, and his second in not contacting the power structure immediately upon being told by the board to seek other employment. When asked by the industrial manager, "What do you want us to do?", the superintendent issued an ultimatum. First, he asked that he be given a new term contract, and, second, that he be given a raise in pay. The members of the power structure, accustomed to seeking compromise alternatives, did not like this response, but they gave no definite answer and told him that they would discuss his situation.

After some deliberation, these community leaders decided against inviting open conflict because of the pride they had in their community. Some of this group were reluctant to abandon the superintendent, however, and discussions between them went on for two or three months. Finally, the choice of letting the superintendent go rather than precipitating an open confrontation was made.

The procedure was as follows:

1. The superintendent would be told that he should resign immediately. They would help him seek employment elsewhere.

2. The most respected men of the group, as well as some of their business subordinates who had community stature, would be asked to write letters to the newspaper commending the superintendent after his resignation for a job very well done. These letters appeared in the paper in conspicuous spots on the editorial page, but only the story of the resignation appeared on the front page. The story included, of course, many laudatory facts about the superintendent's career, the stature of the school nationally, and other complimentary aspects. These letters were concentrated in a period of about a week. The newspaper editor gave the best letters space and published no critical letters.

3. The most respected member of the power group was asked to be chairman of the school board's nominations committee for the coming year. This was satisfactory to the school board who respected the nominee. Unaware of these strategy meetings, the members assumed they had been given support since there was no sign of overt opposition.

4. The chairman of the nominating committee held the meeting at large in the gymnasium of the high school which had been named after him. A committee was selected to recommend candidates for the school board, a procedure that gave virtual control to the power figures, since they had planted the nominations of highly respected members of the community through discussion with their friends on the committee. And, since the choice of a nominating committee is usually not an issue of controversy when there is no apparent conflict, the candidates suggested by the power structure were easily elected.

5. This committee then selected candidates for the

school board, all of them persons who had previously proved cooperative with the members of the power structure, and who neither by virtue of their personalities or business interests could afford to "rock the board." None of the members of the board who had voted to fire the superintendent ran again, and they were on the minority side as soon as the next election occurred.

The next superintendent was carefully chosen from a middle-class community and was known to be especially sensitive to keeping things running smoothly in a setting in which conflict and confrontation were unheard of.

A closer watch was kept on the nominations of the school board members for the next election or two, until the power structure decided that matters were again under control, and returned to their past ways, expecting the board and superintendent to watch out for their interests. The superintendent who had been fired was helped by them to get a very good job in another community, and he did not lose money or prestige in the process.

The new superintendent maintained the low tax rates, and continued the previous policies of hiring graduate student wives as teachers and emphasizing a college preparatory curriculum. The new board members consulted the leadership in the community on crucial issues, but in the main their philosophy did not differ sufficiently to warrant frequent consulting.

We find, then, that in the classical case of the dominated community the school is well run for the most part; only when confrontation accidently arises do we find the power structure intruding into deliberate decision-making. We further find that the superintendent must play the role of the functionary, consistent with the ideology and specific criteria imposed by the power structure, if he is to be supported by these men. It was evident to us that if the power figures had decided to support the superintendent, the members of the board who had voted to fire him would have changed their position immediately. So far as we could determine, none of them had sufficient grounds for maintaining a position against the pressure of such respected sources in the community.

Of course, at the time of the firing, there was much discussion at parties and across the back fence about the reasons for the firing, but there was practically no knowledge of the interplay between the bank vice-president, the bank president, the editor, and the manager of the local industry, or any of the other parties involved in settling the issue. It is significant that there was no question in the minds of the top power figures about who to call to make the decision as to what should be done, nor did they encounter any difficulty in implementing their own decisions. It was the violation of their expectations that caused the members of the power structure to abandon the superintendent when they could have fairly easily arranged to keep him on.

The fact that these persons neither brag about nor deny such events is probably a reflection of the security they feel in their positions. They regard their role as one of protecting the basic mores of the community; in this case, a community dominated by the middle class, and they see their actions as consistent with the values of that class. They do feel somewhat guilty about the privacy of their deliberations, but not overly so since these techniques are consistent with the accepted norms of their occupational life.

CRITERIA OF DOMINATION

We do not at this time find that the failure of a dominant group to succeed in all of its wishes is adequate grounds for rejecting the notion that domination exists in some communities. This is especially so when issues are voted upon; power figures do not appear to us to be public opinion leaders. Nonetheless, when "behind the scenes" manipulation can be used to prevent certain issues from arising, we feel that domination exists—and we found it operating, not only in the community described in the immediately preceding pages, but in others as well.

Because of the running argument over the issue of the existence of domination, we felt that some relatively stringent criteria should be employed—both to come as close as possible to meeting the objections of critics of the reputational method and the "domination" theorists, and to present our own subscription to the theory itself.

Our position is that domination clearly exists in some communities with respect to the educational enterprise. The problem is chiefly one of determining the extent to which a single group of power figures controls the important community decisions regardless of the institutional order.

Generalized domination was found in some communities, but in others whose school affairs were dominated, we failed to find any indication or evidence of generalized domination.

The following interview with a person from a dominated community illustrates the generality of dominant power in the sense that control is *given* to one person to *prevent* certain types of community-wide action. The respondent had recently left the community for a position at the state level, but was still active in local affairs. He had been a member of the school board, a member of the power group, and still had close contacts in the community. The community is a small city in our stratified sample.

> *Interviewer:* Are there any people or groups who are more influential in this community or do most people have about the same influence?
>
> *Respondent:* Oh, yes. In fact, it rests in one man, the banker. Whenever an industry comes into town or even thinks about it, they go to him not only for credit but for guidance. Problems such as where to locate, whether to come in the town or not, and the extent to which they should appeal to certain kinds of workers are all discussed with him thoroughly.
>
> *Interviewer:* If a member of an industry thinking about coming to this community talked to someone else, how would this work?
>
> *Respondent:* Well, that person would send them to this banker. I would not wish to give the impression that this banker comes on strong. None of these fellows do. I work now in several communities where I have to know the most influential people, and I find none of them coming on strong. They are real gentlemen, and quite often fairly quiet men. However, when they have something to say, they say it and people listen.
>
> *Interviewer:* Can you think of any cases where this banker has actually blocked some action in the community?

Respondent: Oh, yes, quite a few. I remember once there was a liquor store located right on the highway which went through the middle of town. It did not have a sign on it. The boys in the Lions Club at lunch discussed it and got pretty excited about letting a community action program put up a sign with community money. They thought that it was not permissible to put up a sign with the store profits because of state law. After about a half an hour, things seemed to be going well and the plans were crystallizing. The banker, who had said nothing up to that time, said, "I think we have a lot of things in the community that need a lot more of our attention than advertising liquor to the public." After that, nothing more was said at all.

Interviewer: Not a thing?

Respondent: Not a thing. Another time, I remember in our church—he is a member of our church—another church wanted to rent our basement for some affair. I watched him and his wife and although they did not say much they were obviously against the rental. After a while, his wife got up and talked for some time, probably two or three minutes, and sat down. I couldn't prove it but I am almost certain that they had talked to some of their friends ahead of time about the matter and agreed. Of course we did not rent the basement to the other church.

Interviewer: What makes you think they talked ahead of time?

Respondent: Well, I was on the school board with him for a long time until I resigned to take this state office. We often got together before the meeting and talked things out. I remember once I had been out of town and came back to learn that one of the boys from a good family in town had to get married to a girl who was also from a good family. The superintendent had talked to the interhigh school league, which has a hard and fast rule that such boys cannot participate in any extra curricular activities. I said that I felt that the superintendent should not have talked to them first but rather come to the board with it. The superintendent never wanted to get involved in anything. He certainly did not want to get involved in an argument over this. He had called several board members before the meeting, and told them that this would come up. I was not there but my wife took the message. The vote was six to one, with my dissent being the only one. My argument was that the boy and girl had suffered enough. Why punish them further? However, everybody else argued pretty much the same point—that this kind of behavior could not be condoned by the school because it might encourage other boys and girls to do the same thing. Although the banker did not say anything in the meeting, I learned from my friends later on that this had been the one thing he had said in the meeting before the public meeting.

Interviewer: Did he hold this against you?

Respondent: Oh, no. He knew I had not been able to meet with them beforehand. Furthermore, he will tolerate disagreement, as long as it does not get violent.

Interviewer: Do you think he is concerned with violence and conflict or not?

Respondent: Oh, yes. I imagine he would compromise on moderately important issues to avoid open conflict in the community. None of us wants that. When I was there, I always called parents or anybody in the community who might raise a stink before any school board meeting to try to get them to come in and present their case in a reasonable manner so that we could discuss it. Conflict is a very unpleasant thing, and anyone, who really has influence in a community where there is strong leadership, will try at almost all cost to eliminate the conflict. Of course you can't always eliminate it, and none of us would sacrifice our most basic beliefs to eliminate it.

Interviewer: Can you think of any other cases where some action was blocked?

Respondent: Yes, just a couple of weeks ago I had an opportunity to get into a new company with very little money and get quite a few stocks in it. I think it's going to be a real go. I went back to my home community and talked to the banker about this and the company said that we had to raise $125,000 for a building and a parking lot and a few things like that. He felt that $125,000 was a little too much for this kind of company and for that size of community right now. I think he's probably getting pretty old and does not want to get involved in anything this chancy when the benefits will be reaped quite a few years from now.

Interviewer: Have you done anything further on the matter?

Respondent: No, and I will not. I'm sure we'll never be able to raise any money there unless he either helps raise it, or gets some of his lieutenants to do this. Don't misunderstand me, I am a very good friend of this man, but I feel that he does control most things in the community. He is a good man, not a bad man, and the control is, I think, a very good thing.

The direct involvement of power figures in the dominated community in educational policy matters seems to vary considerably from one community to another. Hunter found that in Atlanta the top power figures of the community for the most part did not even attend meetings, much less hold office. We found a similar pattern in some of our communities, especially the larger ones. Size is a significant factor. The extent of direct involvement may also be affected by the importance of the school in the local political structure, that is to say, when the school is highly visible to the community at large, dominants may accept posts on the school board.

Three of our most dominated communities showed a direct involvement of top power figures in the school board itself. One of these was a one-industry town, the population of which placed it at the lower end of the small city strata. The industry, a nationally known one, had its headquarters in the city; the city and high school were named after the industry's president and the housing was built by the industry. The president of the school board was the chief attorney for the company, and very soon after the interviews were taken he was made vice-president. The other two members of the three-member board of education were employed by the company. The following interview reflects the single line of control which parallels that of the industry itself.

> *Interviewer:* Are there any particular issues you would be reluctant to bring up before the board?
> *President of the Board:* I don't know of any. We have pretty free discussions. Almost never have a split decision on anything. All three are interested in having a good school to the advantage of the end result.
> *Interviewer:* If you have difficulty in reaching agreement on issues, how are these differences ironed out?
> *President of the Board:* Just by discussion and compromise. The area of disagreement is relatively small. I don't think the differences in opinion are so great. If they do occur we get together and discuss them before the board meeting once in a while.

Another board member's view of that same board reports the same line of control in different language:

> *Interviewer:* If you have difficulty in reaching agreement on issues, how are these differences ironed out?
> *Board Member:* We just look to the director and see

which way his head is nodding. If he seems in favor, we vote yes. If he seems against the proposal, we vote no. It's as simple as that. It's easy to be a school board member here.

The mechanism of control is to keep the board small, since this state allowed an option of from three to seven members on the school board. While the electorate might fail to elect a high-level member from the industry to the school board, the control of nominations in the nominating committee by the school board itself assured that except in times of extreme conflict—which we found no instances of in the entire history of the community—no opposing candidate would be nominated.

The consultation by board members with members of the community's informal power structure has been criticized as ineffective evidence of domination on the grounds that major issues often risk being defeated by voters. It appears to us that the degree of influence community leaders wield over a board and its superintendent is the critical determinant of whether a dominant power structure exists, and not the possible defeat of the desires of certain groups at the polls. It is characteristic of the dominated community that the polls offer about the only resource the citizenry has to defy decisions of the power structure, and since so many decisions are made without a public vote, the opportunity for the silent majority to express itself is rare indeed. The following exchange with one president of a dominated board illustrates this point.

Question: Is there anyone special with whom you would talk in the community?
Answer: Well, this community is loaded with talent. If

there are any people who have political influence we definitely might talk to them, for example, the city fathers, the board of trustees, the village trustees, and we meet with them informally or at their meetings. As you probably know, I was chairman of the committee which steered the school bond issue through. We had been defeated once, which was a shocking thing for most people in this community, but the city fathers felt that our school system should have everything it needed so they asked me to form a committee to review the situation, and we did review it. It took really three years to build an entirely new support program. We put it over finally.

Question: How would you analyze the defeat the first time?

Answer: The defeat was partly because it was improperly sold, partly because the plan evidently was not clearly understood and the need was not clearly understood. It was a good plan, but it wasn't probably presented right and fairly documented. It hadn't been cleared with the right groups and it didn't have enough time to soak in. This time we had a committee on educational needs and a committee translating those needs into engineering and architectural plans. We also had another committee on finance and another committee on presenting it to the public.

Question: These were lay committees, citizens?

Answer: Citizens committees, made up of all the organized groups within the community, and we cleared it in advance with every one of them. We worked very closely, of course, with the trustees of the village and we also worked with a real estate man who pays a great deal of tax here and who had bitterly opposed the previous bond issue. We neutralized him because we had all the important people with us. The public at large usually goes along when it realizes the city fathers are really behind an issue.

Domination is commonly expressed in at least three forms. One is the ideologically dominated community, where the shared philosophy with respect to schools and other matters results in the dominators not having to exert themselves actively. Ideology alone takes care of the decision-making process. The second is the one-industry town, in which the core of the population is employed either in a central industry or in smaller occupations which service the central industry. Here, power is reinforced not by an ideology but by the self-interest of the board member in his occupational setting. In other words, his decisions are made in terms of his advancement and security in his occupational career. A third situation in which the dominated community runs smoothly is the type described in our paradigm case in which there may be a diversity of interests, but where top-level personnel are in total agreement regarding methods. Every attempt is made to avoid conflict, confrontation, and the like. It is only when there is a distracting mixture of roles or structures that it becomes necessary, under the three types of conditions named above, for the power structure to come into open play. The test of domination must therefore await an event which precipitates the exertion of manifest power.

3

THE
MECHANISMS
OF CONTROL

"Big policy" is a term often used to describe the salient issues that draw the top power figures of a community into the decision-making process. Big policy in Atlanta revolved around school matters, welfare issues, taxes, race relations, and labor affairs. A marked difference between our findings and Hunter's with respect to the dominated community is that we believe it useful to view the processes by which control is exercised as identical to "big policy." Maintaining control is of the same order as maintaining low taxes.

The main concern of most top leaders in a dominated community is the avoidance of conflict. Conflict as an end in itself may be relished by some activists, but socially dominant persons try to suppress it: open conflict is simply not considered legitimate in the dominated community.

One dominant was asked: "If conflict arises and gets pretty much out-of-hand, how do you proceed?"

He replied: "Well, clearly, the first thing to do is to

reduce the conflict. Then, if I'm sure that this is taken care of, we might try to figure out how to avoid it in the future."

In those communities in which domination is successful the high priority given to reducing conflict generally results in cultural homogeneity. Various strategies are invoked: ritualistic means of giving vent to frustrations, keeping power plays secret, and defining conflict from pulpit, lectern, and press as morally undesirable. Highly dominant persons are usually willing to pay a high price to educate their children, so long as they can control key policies. If power figures send their children to private schools, they may be less altruistic than those who have their children in the public schools but not necessarily so.

Keeping taxes down is not a negligible matter to dominants, especially in a business community, but the rising costs for able teachers and the demands for new buildings and equipment have forced school board members and those who support them to increase school budgets dramatically. This fact was emphasized by a community power leader in a dominated community in these words: "Our per pupil cost is outrageous but we have decided that our schools are going to be as good or better than any private preparatory school in the country. We know what we want, we have the resources, and we have the will to do the job the way it should be done." It is rather difficult for the citizenry at large to be dissatisfied with schools which are clearly superior.

Individuals who dominate a community naturally wish to maintain the status quo since institutions, agencies, and groups tend to build self-perpetuating devices into their group structure. Small towns are discrete manageable units susceptible to influence from a select few, but the pressure from government to merge small school districts into larger ones has disturbed the old order and created new pressures for consolidation.

Many states practically force school districts to join together by the inducements they offer. Resistance to such pressure has been bitter and sustained in spite of obvious economic disadvantages. This suggests that domination itself, and what that may mean for the protection of unique local mores, is often more important than any financial bonus which might accrue through expanded state aids.

The dominant power structure is not so selfish as to choose poor instead of good education just to maintain a tenuous control. Rather, the school courses deemed by them to be of fundamental importance are offered regardless of cost or inconvenience. Note how an insightful board member describes the situation:

> One of the problems we are going to have in the next few years is joining hands with the nearby village in a consolidated school system. We don't want this, but fortunately for us neither do they. I'm sure that as more people come in from outside there'll be some pressure building up in this community to consolidate in order to provide some courses that we just cannot afford right now because we have too few students interested in them. I suppose what will happen is that either we will have to offer those courses for a very few students or we will be forced to consolidate.

The domination of any community is never altogether complete. Domination is not dictatorship: the "God" complex is not that popular in our society. Even board members and superintendents in the dominated community get phone calls at home protesting policies and, at times, explicit decisions. While the tendency to interfere seems minimal in dominated communities, this perception may be a manifestation of the self-confidence exuded by power figures. The response of the dominated structure to highly vocal and militant opposition is reasonable and peaceful. If there appears to be an honest and effective threat to established ways of operating, conciliatory remedies are introduced, as long as the basic structure is not threatened. Hence, it is apparent that activists are most effective in preventing rather than bringing about change. Sex education curricula and courses on communism are often not implemented by a dominant structure, a constraint caused mainly by the desire to keep temperatures at a low level. Why should a dominant group challenge the prejudices of a minority in areas where it does not care one way or the other?

But even in dominated communities some means of venting disagreements and hostilities must be provided. Quite often the school board and more frequently the superintendent spend considerable time listening to the complaints of individual dissenters. This courteous response defuses the anger of the malcontents and assures them that their voices are being heard. While problems are not necessarily resolved, responses of this kind greatly reduce the threat of public confrontation that might occur were these venting mechanisms not available. The beneficial effects of listening to one's detractors are best expressed in the comments of a newspaper reporter in a dominated community: "The people who run this community are very sophisticated. Even the most stupid character is given a hearing; after he

has been through the soft-soap routine he has been completely mollified. The light touch is practiced to perfection
here."

The dominated board, as any board, has at its disposal
the technique of the executive session to avoid open and
public controversy. It is probable that the dominated board
uses this technique more often than others. To the extent
that certain issues might arouse opposition and therefore
conflict, the dominated board seeks to avoid a public clash.
One member of a dominated board said, when asked whether
there were any subjects he would not wish to bring up in
open session:

> Oh, yes, there are many issues that we would not want to
> discuss in a public meeting. What I mean is that there
> are many controversial issues, none of which we would be
> hesitant to talk about at our executive sessions, but we
> would not wish to discuss them publicly. We intentionally
> avoid public discussions on the subject of race, since this
> community already gets a lot of publicity about it. In
> executive sessions we have a full discussion. We have had
> a number of public board sessions on curriculum, and
> this is healthy, but there are certain aspects, preliminary
> aspects, that we would obviously not discuss openly for
> the simple reason that newspaper reporters are there and
> this might be harmful to the school in the long run.

The secretive nature of the executive session makes it
all the more difficult to assess how the dominated board
operates. While we may view board meetings publicly, and
even obtain data on meetings between board members and
community leaders easily, the executive session is sacrosanct.
Each board member is reluctant to let the public know what
takes place in a secret decision. The following excerpts from

an interview with a board member in a dominated board, in a dominated community, is suggestive of the wide range of functions such executive sessions may have:

> We had this problem of an old school in which there were many Negroes, and it was suggested that we discontinue that school. The community lined up on both sides, and everybody felt pretty strongly about it. We had several public meetings; all we did was listen. We had many closed meetings. In a committee of the whole meeting where no one else was present we discussed it ourselves and finally we made up our minds what we wanted to do, which was close the school. There were a lot of factors involved, it was not just Negroes. We recognized that the school building was a fire trap. I'm sure if the matter had happened a couple of years later, the trouble would have been even more. After we made up our minds, we had a public meeting and you would have had to be there to believe it. The opponents of our plan were very outspoken, oh, they were terrible, and the ones that were for the plan were polite and later everybody got up and started yelling, you had to see something like that to believe it. It is sort of like a scene in a movie which is exaggerated to try to make the point that mob psychology really works. There were so many people there we had to adjourn and go to the auditorium. A lot of the people thought we were being pressured by the NAACP and that's not true. But you had to put all the factors together, and we had to do this in private session . . . well, for instance, to take another tack to show you what you can do in private that you cannot do in public. You build a school and you have problems with the contractor and there is the important question of accepting the school and releasing the funds. It's sort of a war of nerves between the school board and the contractor, and if you have to do all your talking in public so that he knows what your thinking is, you've lost your position.

You may think there that we were unanimous in caucus because in public we usually are. Maybe the vote in committee will be seven to two but when we get out on the public platform we vote unanimously because it's all settled anyway.

Almost every community has a myriad of organizations. If one of these organizations, no matter how low its status, decides to move determinedly in a certain direction, it can bring influence to bear on power figures. This does not mean that the existence of one or two active organizations endangers community domination, that is unless these organizations can mobilize still other groups into a cohesive force. Rather, their presence calls for able process management from those in charge. Frequently it is the school board president who acts to mute these demands; no change takes place but the organization is granted a respectful hearing. The issue is, so to speak, processed to death.

As one respondent said,

The school board president in this community needs to have a lot of political ability and good balance. He must be diplomatic. He must be knowledgeable. I mean, there are certain ingredients that go to make up a person whom you recognize as a leader. We have X number of dollars to spend. We have a budget. And quite often you get some group that wants more than its share. The school board president has to sit down with these groups and explain the situation. It takes quite a bit of diplomacy to sit down with the various groups and explain to them why they will have to wait a year or two.

The reaction of newspapers to school board decisions is of such a dynamic character that it must, in the dominated community, be muzzled in some fashion. The power-

ful influence of the newspaper on the majority of the
population in any community is a constant threat to the
tranquillity of dominants. Hence we frequently find newspaper editors firmly embraced by the power structure. One
newspaper editor, when asked point blank whether board
members sought his opinion in advance of crucial decisions,
answered with an unhesitating yes.

In one community, indicated by every respondent to be
strongly Republican, the editor seemed quite popular with
the Democrats. His explanation was simplicity personified:
"Oh, they like me very much, and especially when I take
a whack at the Republicans on the school board they enjoy
it very much." This quotation gives some indication of the
immediate danger facing a school board member who gets
"out of line."

The empty ritual of board meetings where school
boards are dominated was underlined by the meager attendance at those meetings. Although ostensibly the meetings
were wide open to the public, very few people came. People
are unlikely to spend much time in meetings they think will
not result in changes they want.

Governing elites consciously employ mechanisms at
regularly scheduled meetings to inhibit interest and discour-
age attendance. One dominated board in a dominated community reported that its favorite technique was to begin its
sessions with a rash of activities involving such distractions
as a staff lecture and musical presentations. After these pre-
liminaries, the first matter discussed involved small routine
expenditures—by law a function of the board, but one
which need not take up much time. When the board did
finally get around to an issue in which the public might

be interested, it was quite late in the evening. In this dominated board in which no actual debate was reported by anyone on the board, nor observed by the interviewers, meetings lasted from eight until twelve or twelve-thirty. Whether the mechanism of controlling the agenda by prolonging meetings is in all cases deliberate, its effect is to greatly decrease attendance and participation by the public.

If control is intended, it follows that it is of paramount importance to monitor nominations of board members. In some dominated communities, top leadership has resolved this problem by developing a nominating committee which selects a single slate of board candidates for whom the community votes. For a relatively powerless group to succeed in getting a candidate on the board it must first penetrate the nominating committee. Usually these committees are very large, and it is difficult to get reform candidates on the single list they present to the community for election. The only practical alternative is to run against the preferred slate; to win under such circumstances is next to impossible.

The reports we have on the operation of these nominating committees suggest that they make a publicly observed effort to select people from diverse backgrounds. However, the particular people picked to represent a certain segment of the community, a minority group, or a political or religious affiliation, are not partisan oriented. In a dominated community only "safe" candidates pass the nominating committee's screening tests.

In the absence of a nominating committee, the board ordinarily does its own recruiting. In the dominated community, the replacement of a board member by the board itself is not an infrequent occurrence. In one, a newspaper

editor who had been named as an influential community
figure characterized the process in this fashion:

> *Interviewer:* Suppose a man wanted to become a board
> member in this community. Could you give me your ideas
> on the qualifications he would need and the process he
> would need to go through to become a board member?
> *Respondent:* No. 1, he would have to be a Republican.
> No. 2, he would have to see whoever the local leaders are
> and get their OK or he could run independently if he
> wishes and takes his chances, but an independent seldom
> ever wins.
> *Interviewer:* Are there any groups of local leaders or
> does he have to see some key people here?
> *Respondent:* About two or three key people. His com-
> mitteeman, and the committee chairman, but most of the
> people that are serving on the board now were not origi-
> nally elected. There would be a vacancy and the board
> would fill the vacancy. They come up for reelection and
> they are automatically elected.

The tendency of dominated boards in some communities to select their own members is invited by state statutes
which prescribe that persons who resign, leave the community, or die are replaced by the board itself as an interim
appointment until the next election. The board members
see this as an opportunity to keep people on the board who
act consistent with its aims and methods. As one board member explained it:

> Customarily, vacancies on the school board only occur due
> to an individual moving out of the district, or the death or
> resignation of a member. Under Pennsylvania law, school
> board members can fill a vacancy by their own choice. This
> member then runs later in a regular election. The board

has various selection procedures; sometimes we have knowledge about an individual who is interested in being on the board. Other times we have interviewed as many as twenty to thirty people. The community is about four or five to one Republican; the feeling is that we should only elect a person who we feel will be reelected so that they can become a permanent member of the board. That is why all of our members are Republican. If the board should fill a vacancy with a Democrat, it would be a very temporary situation and the danger would be that at the general election the Republican party would then name some individual that the party had chosen who would not necessarily be consistent with the goals and interests of the school board. We try to eliminate that possibility by electing a Republican that we choose and stay with him. We would not take someone who was extremely devoted to low taxes nor would we take an educator who might be at the other extreme.

The tendency to avoid people directly connected with the educational system itself—school administrators and teachers in other districts as well as college professors—is noted throughout the interviews. These so-called educationists are deemed to be too idealistic and ill equipped to face real problems.

If domination is to occur in a community it must be capable of repressing conflict. As we have outlined, this works best when people who might be in disagreement know that their efforts to change the system would have no effect upon events.

Domination is easier to accomplish in small towns; the very intimacy of relationships forces an attempt at harmony. Further, techniques used to stamp out deviance

(executive sessions, self-perpetuating boards, rambling meetings) ordinarily are successful.

Board members in dominated communities represent
whatever powers are in control; their policies tend to express
the values associated with those in charge. The men who
exercise control over community affairs are particularly
sensitive to the dangers of prolonged controversy and seek
every means to maintain the status quo. Change is slow and
incremental.

The muckraker concept of the evil big business tycoon
lurking in the shadows waiting to punish those who dispute
his hegemony is, of course, a ridiculous caricature. Domination today is a highly sophisticated, perhaps unconscious,
mechanism for enhancing one set of values against those
preferred by someone else. Because of the skill and essentially public posture of those who dominate, the resultant
effect may be much stronger and more pervasive than the
exercise of overt pressure.

4

THE
CARETAKER

Some psychologists would agree that each individual is to an extent unique, that his behavior is partially unpredictable, and that, moreover, he is not consciously aware of many of the motivations which trigger his decisions in new and un-structured situations. While such a set of theoretical principles posits a form of non-Skinnerian anarchy, men in executive positions must give definitive responses to challenges and conflicts without regard to personality differences or cultural dispositions. Because of the circumstances, Commander Bucher had to decide whether to surrender the *Pueblo* to North Korea or not: there was no time to call a committee meeting and seek consensus.

It has become fashionable of late, even approximating cultism, to attempt to modify administrative behavior by various forms of sensitivity training. Is it possible to change significantly the actual behavior of superintendents or their approach to the human problems they face? Whether sensitivity training infuses the executive with authenticity in his relationships with associates is open to question, but few challenge the fundamental assumpton that an individual can be made more aware of his personal impact on other human beings. The remarkable success of brainwashing experiments testifies to the plasticity of the human organism under stress. Although we do not wish to contend that men are simply robots who are endlessly manipulated by environmental constraints, we are equally confident that individuals are not completely free of organization and community influence. Obviously intensity of response to these stimuli or the exercise of initiative under pressure will vary with the individual. Yet, over a wide range of individuals, definite patterns of administrative behavior may be systematically charted.

As organizational structures, schools can be classified as open rather than closed systems. Community institutions continuously interact with the school social system. No boundary line excludes the non-professional. Contrast the fluidity of this arrangement with the mystifying paraphernalia set up by the medical profession to prevent the patient and his family from understanding the reality of hospital management.

In local public schools even the classroom teacher is subject to direct interventions from parents if things do not go as expected. The administrators, and particularly the superintendent of schools, are constantly reminded that evaluation of the educational process is everybody's prerogative. There are no special trappings or recognized expertness in any school system to restrict the layman in his appraisal of the quality of educational experiences. Community demands simply cannot be sloughed off as minor irritants.

As a consequence, school superintendents are particularly vulnerable and expendable bureaucrats. They are enmeshed in local political structures much like city managers. School systems are expensive tax-supported institutions whose costs are mushrooming. Moreover, citizens are able to monitor budget increases in local government much more effectively than in state and federal agencies. The productivity of the educational enterprise is difficult to measure in any quantitative sense (if its objectives are broadly conceived); there is no profit and loss statement to fall back on.

The growing militancy of teacher unions upsets the time-honored proverb that the superintendent represents the teachers' interests to the board of education. He is management whether he wishes it or not. Needless to say, the personal values of a determined set of citizens (i.e., the advisability of sex education or driver training) may be more enforceable directly or indirectly in the local community arena. Caught in the crossfire of these realities, a superintendent of schools is obliged to choose how he will act if conflict arises. It is our contention that there are at least a few who consciously, or unconsciously, solve this dilemma by succumbing to the dominant ethos.

In fact, under a system where the board of education selects its own chief executive it is entirely reasonable to conjecture that the screening process results in a perfect match, in the ideological sense. Under such circumstances a superintendent might agree with the dominant philosophy espoused locally and willingly serve as its visible standard bearer. Another likely speculation is that any perceptive administrator with career ambitions shies away from challenging entrenched forces if he knows he cannot win in the event of a confrontation. Rather than become a martyr, such a person is more likely to seek a more compatible school system as the wisest course to follow. To opt out is less threatening than dismissal or defeat.

It should be emphasized that no elitist group is so repressive that it reduces its superintendent to puppet status. Most operating decisions are perfunctory and even a few minor errors in judgment are likely to be excused. The occasion when expectations are made explicit is rare. Because the boundary limits are tacitly understood, it is not necessary to marshal overt naked power. In fact, if such entanglements do occur, it signifies that domination is not secure. Nor is there any implication that functionaries manage poor schools; domination by enlightened but paternalistic men may result in an excellent organization by most standards. The superintendent is just not free to suggest those alternatives in opposition to established community mores. In the contest between order and freedom, order wins.

Finally, it should be observed that the functionary or caretaker role may well be played by many administrators because it is the easiest course to follow. Research on the roles of school superintendents consistently indicates that most of his average working day is spent in niggling tasks, not in creative or innotative activities. It is up to the superintendent to maintain the system and, as in most enterprises, routine presses inexorably down on the person in charge, the chief executive. He attends meetings, mediates or mutes personnel conflicts, appears at ceremonial functions, answers the telephone, answers his correspondence, supervises financial matters, and the like. Since we also know that schools are understaffed at the top level (research and planning staffs are rare), only a very well-organized and energetic man is likely to free himself from the bonds imposed by the daily travail. Lassitude may account for much of the behavior we describe as that of the functionary.

Where is one most likely to find a functionary as superintendent of schools? Our evidence indicates that homogeneous small communities with single industries invariably produce this behavioral pattern. Such places are likely to employ young inexperienced local men who are relatively docile or maintain in office an old-timer who has proved his reliability in the past. Another instance may be found in factional communities where the majority on the board of education exercises its will so severely that the school superintendent must acquiesce or be hounded out of office. In short, the dominance of the controlling faction is so complete as to rule out strategic compromise. Blatant domination leads inevitably to counter resistance; the fate of the superintendent in such instances is sealed. He is ejected when the new group gets into office.

Finally, wherever one finds a dominated community power structure and a dominated board, we predict that the superintendent who stays in office will act as an agent of this dominance. He really has no other alternative. Kozol's descriptive account of the Boston superintendent explains the role perfectly:

> I refer to Superintendent Ohrenberger as a "good-hearted football coach." He holds an unearned doctoral degree from Calvin Coolidge College. At the time that he was chosen Superintendent, the Harvard Education School consultant,

Dr. Herold Hunt, had recommended six candidates from outside of Boston ahead of him. Within the terms of Boston, of our schools and colleges, athletics and politics, he has been a great success. In a sense he seems a typical prize-winning product of the kinds of schools he now runs. The only question is whether such a man, shaped by such a system and delimited by it, can find the scope to revitalize it and the intellect to give it meaning. Seeing him and hearing him that night, it was difficult to believe he could.[1]

Case studies describing forms of community control over school authorities are unlimited. For purposes of illustration, let us examine briefly two rather different organizational experiences in which the same phenomena under consideration here were studied. Springdale (Candor, New York) is a good example of a community dominated by rural interests rather than town preferences. Further, prosperous farmers, not marginal ones, held the power reins in the community; significantly, the board of education was heavily populated by prosperous farmers. Vidich and Bensman were quick to point out that a rural orientation had consequences for the overall administration and character of the school.[2] The school administrator, Mr. Peabody, was a man of considerable talents. (Incidentally, he now has his doctorate from a major university and is well placed in educational circles.) If by "running a school" we mean the day-to-day maintenance activities, then he ran the school. In fact, he was more than a step ahead of the community in advocating innovations. By most objective standards he would be given good marks as an administrator. Still, when pressed, it is stated that "he agrees most, in terms of his rhetoric, with the rural interests since this is the dominant group within and through which he must work." [3]

Whether a particular school administrator is essentially a functionary depends on the salience of an issue. Does he fight for his own position in arenas which are potentially explosive? Naturally some individuals are by inclination more servile than others. Mr. Peabody clearly had the situation well in hand; he knew the limits of his authority but the important point to remember is that he did not challenge the establishment in those areas where he knew he could not win without considerable risk. To a degree than he was a functionary by choice, since he was using Springdale as a springboard to a higher station.

One might rightfully question whether Vidich and Bensman correctly portrayed Mr. Peabody. Research about power relationships can be criticized on the basis that the perceptions of the observer are value laden and to that degree inaccurate. In our own work we tried to avoid this basic difficulty by crosschecking the impressions of several independent observers, but still we are faced with the fact that complex human behavior is extremely difficult to quantify.

Even new communities with initial homogenous populations do not escape the tendency to seek safe and dependable school administrators who can be counted on to follow established customs. Herbert Gans indicates that the Levittown (New Jersey) school board quickly gave the responsibility for course content, teaching methods, and staff recruitment to the local county superintendent of schools because "the board was familiar with his ideas and meth-

ods and trusted him to design a school system it would find
acceptable." [4] The board of education did not envisage the
development of a lighthouse school system and it chose a
superintendent who agreed with this philosophy. A low-
pressure student-oriented approach to education was insti-
tuted. All went well until an influx of parents with Ivy
League aspirations insisted on early admission to kinder-
garten. Gradually opposition mounted and the superintendent resigned due to "his inability to adapt his previously
rural experience to the wishes of the suburbanites." [5]

At this point it may be useful to restate one of our
fundamental premises. If a superintendent's style of performance does not adjust to the community power structure
and the board's performance expectations, the administrator
may lose his office by voluntary means such as resignation,
but if necessary he will be summarily dismissed. In the case
of Levittown, New Jersey, the first superintendent was a
model functionary. His goals and those of his board members were identical. The first residents were quite happy
with the school system and accepted the superintendent's
laissez-faire attitude toward achievement with little dissent.
But as more affluent citizens took up residence in Levittown
it changed rather drastically from domination to factionalism and the incumbent superintendent was unable to play
the more delicate role of political strategist. Suffice it to say
that a functionary, whose role may seem safe and secure in
the theoretical sense, is equally vulnerable if the community
power structure changes. In a stable situation the functionary could be expected to last until retirement if he so wished.

Osopeachy is a small compact village located a few

miles from Big City. Wealth is everywhere evident. Maids
are likely to answer the door or the telephone. The shops are
selective and expensive. The public buildings are a far cry
from the run-down nineteenth-century fire traps characteristic of many of the drab communities in the northeast.
The Osopeachy Police Station, for instance, could easily be
mistaken for a country club. Osopeachy's wealth is produced
by a large group of executive-class men who work in top
positions in Big City. The school system itself is small; the
teaching staff numbers less than one hundred and is extremely well paid.

The striking thing about Osopeachy is its peculiar in-
sularity. It is an island of privilege; perhaps like a medieval
fortress. Within the walls, everything is ordered and controlled according to a certain viewpoint, and that viewpoint
is bolstered by money, talent, and tradition. Members of the
community do venture into the larger world and they operate effectively in it. But the values they confront in their jobs
and travels and outside associations are not the same values
they insist on within their own community. Osopeachy is
dominated by a rigidly conservative Republican doctrine
which would classify it in the eyes of some as one of the
last real WASP enclaves. Except for a small pocket of dissenters, domestics, and other members of the working class
who comprise the smallest segment of the population, the
community's unifying theme is that of an "ethnically sheltered
island community."

The school board's seven members are elected for
three-year terms, though "elected" is not an accurate term.
Rather, the members are selected by a non-partisan self-

perpetuating nominating committee; being tapped by the committee assures election. Osopeachy prides itself, in fact, on being "non-political" on educational issues.

At one time the school system was considered to be very progressive; it was one of the original members of the famous Eight-Year Study. At present preparing students for college entrance is its main preoccupation. Osopeachy is a good, solid, academically respectable place which does not experiment until practices have proven out elsewhere.

Osopeachy is an ideal example of domination by ideology, the most pervasive of all forms of control. There is tremendous unity of thought in the community—Little Rock was not nearly so united—and there is a large reservoir of talent. One might at first think that the community was pluralistic in nature, but in truth this rich, conservative, church-oriented, high-level business group controls the direction of the school program to a greater extent than even it realizes. Still, the vehicle for this domination is the nonpartisan nominating committee which is self perpetuating in that it replaces board members with its own kind. The community is satisfied with its uncontested board elections. For example, there are 3,300 eligible voters, but in most school elections the vote is between twenty-five and eighty-five people.

The leadership capacities of the superintendent in Osopeachy were discussed by one of our respondents in these terms:

> *Interviewer:* Does your superintendent have the authority to go with his responsibility?
> *Respondent:* I personally feel that he should be in that position but I also personally feel that he is not capable

of taking the initiative. I don't think this particular superintendent is ever going to be an innovator.

Interviewer: You're saying that he is not a first-rate educational leader?

Respondent: I am regretfully coming to that conclusion.
You have to look at the whole picture and then decide
where the blame is. I think that we are getting drearier
and drearier teachers.

Interviewer: In spite of the very attractive salary sched-
ules?

Respondent: Yes, this interests me, I don't know why. I
know that in the elementary school nobody ever asks us
what we are doing anymore. No one ever asks our Osopeachy
elementary school to send representatives to conferences to
say what Osopeachy is doing because we aren't doing anything, so we have had a lot of teacher turnover.

Interviewer: Is it true that the superintendent has to go
along with the wishes of the board and community or
they will throw him out?

Respondent: Exactly, that's right. Although I do think
some very able school administrators have fought the
wishes of the community and held their jobs. Look at
Harold Howe. He was hired by a school board, but he
couldn't care less what the community thought if he thought
they were wrong. He had certain ideas about education.

Interviewer: Are you commending him for this?

Respondent: I'm remarking that it didn't hurt his career.
You should lead the community; the community should
not lead the administration because I don't think the community is qualified to know what's going on. We are all
doing other things.

Another community influential put the general community position rather bluntly:

Interviewer: How about if the superintendent made some

decisions which you felt were for the good of the school
but were unpopular in the community; how would you
react to him?

Respondent: That's a little difficult to say, but I suppose
if we are looking at this from a theoretical point of view I
would have to fall back on the idea that the board is responsible for making policy and he is the executive in this
case, so if he were becoming outspoken, defiant, independent and running counter to the general board policy I
would tend to go along with the board and the community
in the theoretical sense.

While the superintendent may be a functionary, he is
not an abject tool. He is reported to be an intelligent if not
imaginative person. No rational man would make a habit
of direct confrontation with this board and anyone would
be liable to feeling intimidated at times before this group.
The board respects reasonable and solid recommendations
within the tolerances that are visible for all to witness. While
the superintendent is somewhat overawed by the intellectual
power of the board, he is respected by the board for the strategic way in which he resolves most operational problems.

Textbooks on administration tend to exhort the executive to initiate structure, to take forceful positions, to
mobilize political support, to change the organization by
sheer personal charisma. Such a charge has quite an attrac-
tion to the uninitiated, but is it feasible? We would answer
that in a dominated community with a dominated board, it
would be nearly impossible.

It is interesting to contrast the pose of institutional
maintenance of the Osopeachy superintendent with a superintendent in another eastern state in a similar kind of community. This superintendent's behavior was described by

one of his board members in these terms: "He is much more vocal than he should be. He is a very competitive person. He makes no attempt to disguise how he feels about any issue."

This particular superintendent has long since departed his post; he obtained a first-rate superintendency in a nationally known school system in the Midwest, where he immediately ran into trouble and was fired by his board of education. The innovator in an ideologically dominated community needs to be very secure psychologically, as he is certain to become the center of controversy and he may very well be forced out of office.

In a dominated community, the superintendent is always exposed to the possibility of a factional situation if the teachers are active and organized. Such a probability is becoming more common than uncommon. To the extent that superintendents are dependent upon the approval of state education departments and teacher training institutions for security in case of the necessity of an involuntary resignation, they must be careful not to step outside the limits of their supervisory roles in their relationships with teachers. When the teachers and the dominated community and board find important differences, the superintendent is caught in a conflict situation where both sides are crucial to his life chances. This point is especially important in implementing the long-standing policy in educational organizations, that a supervisor must protect his subordinates at all costs. On the other hand, subordinates generally do not become overly distressed if the superintendent is fired. Like baseball managers, it is all part of the game. We found this unusual form of masochistic self-destruction to be a major cause of involuntary resignation on the part of superintendents who had, in the past, played the role of functionary, except in cases where the principle of protecting subordinates and teachers, came into play. One community leader, a past member of the school board, cited such an incident. He discussed a circumstance that occurred when he was on the board, in which a teacher's job was saved only by tenure laws. In reporting this event, the community leader said that it had not been his place to become involved in personnel matters, but he was upset. He said further:

> I told the teacher what I thought of him, what the board thought of him, and what the community thought of him. At the time we had a superintendent who was a very, very able principal. He had been principal of a high school in another town, I believe, before he became a superintendent here. He was employed here as a superintendent of our school system. Well, there is a great deal of difference between the job of principal and that of a superintendent, as you well know, and he could not cope with the personnel problems and that's the main part of his job. He just couldn't do it. He could not stand to think that somebody that was working in the system wasn't perfect. I asked him for a report on each member of the staff along with his recommendations, and at that time we had about 120 teachers and there wasn't one that he didn't believe was better than an average teacher. At least he would not put it in writing. Now when you talked to him it was a little bit different but he would never put anything in writing that way. He was afraid of his own personnel. He followed the path of least resistance. Well, as a result, our system was getting worse, and worse, because as I explained, we were building up and retaining poor personnel, and some of our good personnel were leaving and each time he replaced them we were getting someone not as good. Well, it

ended up by the superintendent being asked to leave, and
he did leave, and at the time that he left we also got rid of
four or five or six of the teachers that were the poorest.

Interviewer: How did that come about? Did they just
voluntarily leave?"
Answer: Well, yes, they left voluntarily because they
were told that they were going to be fired, and rather than
fight it out, which they could have done, because we would
have had a great deal of difficulty in firing them even
though they were incompetent, inasmuch as our own superintendent would never have testified that they were
incompetent. He was afraid of the teachers.

The influence of mass society, of highly vocal individual parents, of the increasing organization and militancy of
teachers, and other self-interested groups, leads to a situation
in which almost all superintendents may have to use tactics
characteristic of the political strategist. It is not enough in
these situations to simply "go with the system." When
various groups around the superintendent are, in their own
domain, dominant groups, that become conflict-oriented
when they meet (for example, a dominated community con-
fronting an ideologically dominated state education department supported by teacher-training institutions), each group
may expect the superintendent to "exert leadership" by
which they mean, taking an active role in furthering the
educational policies espoused by their group.

Such an expectation is exhibited in another excerpt
from the interview previously referred to in which the superintendent had been fired because he supported the teachers
against the board: "We have a new superintendent now and
we have a more aggressive system now because we have a

man who leads the system." It was in this community that we found the greatest distinction between competent and incompetent teachers. The rewards to the competent and the pressures on the incompetent were articulated clearly and appeared to be effective in keeping the kind of personnel desired by the community power structure and by the board.

Still another feature of the role of the functionary is that he may be required to take postures that give the outward pretense of strong leadership when in reality he is being sharply circumscribed. Indeed, in the most dominated community of our sample, we found the superintendent classified by our judges as a professional adviser. He was a professional adviser because that was the role assigned to him by the community and the board, and because he had been given the knowledge that the previous superintendents had been forced to resign when they did not play this role. That his professional decisions were somewhat less than advisory is indicated in the following example:

> The board makes policy, and the superintendent carries it out. When I was on the board, the superintendent came to us one night and said, "We are going to drop Latin." "Well, why are we going to drop Latin?" "Well," he said, "it is hard to get a teacher." "But," I said, "we're teaching it." So our policy was made that night. The policy was this: We were not dropping Latin. It is a part of the curriculum of this school system. You either find a capable instructor or we'll find somebody that can find a capable instructor. This was the one we asked for a resignation.

The very next words of this same respondent, however, indicated that the professional adviser's role was now demanded:

When I first came on the board, the first week, the superintendent sat out here in the reception room with two people and I was busy. He invited them in and said it wouldn't take very long and said he wanted me to meet them. They were the candidates for this job and that job. I said, "Well, why did you bring them in here?" "Well," he said, "I want you to meet them," and I said, "I don't want to meet them, that's your job." I told him, "I'm not an employer. I know nothing about employing teachers. That's your job. That's what you're being paid for."

The interviewer then asked, "Well, how about the superintendent that you have today? Is it the same situation with him?" The respondent answered, "Oh, he employs them. Sure. That was all stopped immediately."

The delegation of authority is another factor that often leads to the role of professional adviser being subsumed by the functionary. The practice in major industries to delegate authority carries over when big businessmen assume school board positions. This point was made lucidly by a community leader in a community dominated by national firms:

I personally think that the selection of textbooks should be left one hundred percent to the faculty. By that I mean the teachers should recommend it to their superiors, and then it should go on up the line. It should be decided by the professional group. We do not feel that any school board member should say, "Well, we do not like that book, or we don't like this book," because we are not trained to determine that. That's why we have a principal and a superintendent. If the book turns out to be poor, it's their neck.

Thus, the school board has a responsibility to the citizenry parallel to that a board of directors in a corporation has to its stockholders. The management makes the decision upon the advice of professionally trained specialists who are under them. If general failure is found, in this case the selection of poor or undesirable textbooks, the board has the option of firing the management responsible for the decision. General approaches are prescribed but tactics are left to the person who must do the job. Consistent with the success of this mode of operation in their own businesses, the superintendent was delegated authority but not responsibility, and the board members knew the difference.

We agree with a comment by an interviewer who reported on this particular case.

> The superintendent could be classified as a professional adviser. He is a professional adviser to a certain extent because the board relies on him and expects him to get educational research and theory translated into alternatives from which the board may then choose. He is no doubt a functionary in the sense that he just does his job as the board sees his job; but the board see his job as that of a professional adviser. There is no doubt, however, that if he were to make a bad administrative decision, bad in the eyes of board members, he would be fired. However, if he lucks out, he will be rewarded by pay increments, and a possible position with the state department of education.

The superintendent of schools in a dominated community with a dominated board is reasonably secure in his position as long as he does not violate the values preeminent in his community. If he is professionally competent, for even dominated situations will not tolerate outright mismanagement, incremental improvements are possible through carefully planned changes properly approved by those who control the resources. Revolutionary doctrines or rapid moves are likely to be discouraged; however, over time a superintendent can gain the confidence of his community and be trusted to perform his role without excessive interference. The important thing to remember is that the superintendent must be perceptive enough to analyze his degrees of freedom; he is well advised to keep both ears to the ground.

Lindblom has summed up in positive terms the administrative behaviors performed by a caretaker administrator:

> On superficial examination they are often dismissed as irrational. For they are seen as indecisiveness, patching up, timidity, triviality, narrowness of view, inconclusiveness, caution, and procrastination. The piecemealing, remedial incrementalist of satisfier may not look like an heroic figure. He is nevertheless a shrewd, resourceful problem solver who is wrestling bravely with a universe that he is wise enough to know is too big for him.[6]

Up to now, we have been careful not to make judgments about what a superintendent's behavior *should* be. This is a value question that has been vigorously debated: Plato does not square with Machiavelli nor Hobbes with Weber. What we do state unequivocally is that the superintendent's behavior is substantially influenced by the environment in which he works. The purpose of this chapter has been to relate one form of his adaptation.

NOTES

1. Jonathan Kozol, *Death at an Early Age,* Boston: Houghton Mifflin, 1967, p. 240.

2. Arthur J. Vidich and Joseph Bensman, *Smalltown in Mass Society: Class, Power, and Religion in a Rural Community,* Princeton: Princeton University Press, 1958, p. 329.

3. Ibid., p. 200.

4. Herbert J. Gans, *The Levittowners: Ways of Life and Politics in a New Suburban Community,* New York: Random House, 1967, pp. 71–81, 86.

5. Ibid., p. 99.

6. Charles E. Lindblom, *The Policy Making Process,* Englewood Cliffs, New Jersey: Prentice Hall, 1968, p. 122.

PART THREE

THE FACTIONAL COMMUNITY, THE FACTIONAL BOARD, AND THE SUPERINTENDENT AS POLITICAL STRATEGIST

When large and well organized factions rise to face power figures, at least two pyramids of power develop. Often, such confrontation has been so repressed that the rhetoric of suspicion, hate, and personal vendetta which accompanies its release results in a relatively permanent structure in which community factions line up against each other on almost every issue of any importance.

If a faction is to have its way, it must control community-wide boards, such as the board of education. Therefore, elections become arenas in which the factional contest is fought out, year after year. Whichever faction is in the majority controls as if it were a dominating force—except that such control may last only until the next election.

If the superintendent is to accomplish anything educationally, he must cooperate with the majority. But if he does this wholeheartedly, he may lose his job after the next election, when this year's minority becomes the majority—thus his role must be one of political strategist.

5

SUSTAINED
FACTIONS

Almost everyone would agree that interest groups exist in our society, a phenomenon often held up as dynamic evidence of the vitality of American political institutions. That some communities become divided on school issues is a fact hardly worth documenting. It is part of our creed that special interest groups should have the right and even the responsibility to champion their unique causes. It is our contention that some communities sustain persistent conflict between two or three large factions over relatively long periods of time and that these factions are relatively consistent in membership. These factions also maintain a recognizable posture toward most basic issues in the community.

Many of the larger cities in the United States (New York City, for example) are classic illustrations of factional communities, one of the main reasons they are also impossible to govern systematically. As our paradigm case, however, we have selected a smaller city of slightly less than 100,000 population. The large majority of the population are in the lower middle-class income and reside in relatively new but look-alike ranch-style houses; a few upper middle-class professionals and businessmen reside in a special enclave. The community is new, and since the school district overlaps with many governmental subdivisions there is little opportunity for the expression of political ambition at the local community level other than through the school board. Therefore, to become a candidate for the school board is to announce one's availability for office in the state legislature and other political arenas, unlike other communities where a political career might be launched through mayoral candidacy, running for the city council, or the office of prosecuting attorney.

The homogeneous class background of the population might lead one to believe that it would not be factional; however, the presence of large Jewish and Catholic populations leads to sharply contrasting approaches to education. The permissive Jewish attitude versus the traditional Catholic one has generated a dispute of national proportions. We found at one point that approximately one hundred teachers, all members of the teachers' union, had signed a full-page advertisement in the largest city paper in the area to proclaim that they were looking for jobs elsewhere because of the conservative decisions the majority was handing down.

This is not to say that there were not complex issues and problems besetting the schools in this district, due to the rapid population growth and an unusual amount of difficulty in tax assessments, in obtaining new buildings, and in hiring new teachers.

Essentially two groups were vying for control, with the support of each so evenly divided that every election might see the triumph of one group over the other. Campaigns for school board membership were unusually vitriolic. Vulgar posters were sent out by each side accusing the other of lies in language that left no room for doubt: when someone was accused of telling a lie, the word lie was used. On the surface, the campaigns were fought over taxes, but the issue of taxes only served to focus sharp splits in attitudes toward educational philosophy, the amount of money to be used in new buildings, the name of a school, and the like. Because there was little opportunity for power to operate in the dominated style, we discovered that people high in the power structure of each faction themselves ran for the school board.

Much of the campaign literature plainly stated or hinted at personal attacks on the integrity, religious affiliation, and personalities of the opposing candidate. The religious identification of Jews and Catholics was exploited in a number of ways. Catholics were accused of trying to undermine the public schools by insisting that the King James' version of the Bible should not be used, in an effort to take religion out of the public schools and thereby preserve a rationale for the expensive parochial school system which many of them could not afford to support. On the other hand, Catholics insisted that the parochial schools had better discipline, placed more emphasis on moral training, effected economics in operation which did not detract from educational opportunity, and advanced the idea that there is closer contact between Catholic schools and parents. Accusations were added concerning the misuse of expense account funds for personal use. The local press used unusually provocative words in their headlines.

When we arrived on the scene, the faction in the majority had just changed, the liberals had lost the election to the conservatives. The superintendent who had been cooperating with the liberal majority, and doing so with more vigor than is usually found in a political strategist, was fired at the first meeting by the new majority. Consultation with the state education department indicated that this action might not have been too wise, and he was reinstated at the next meeting. At the third meeting, however, he was fired again, and this time it was final. In hiring a new superintendent, the majority selected a person who was weak, who probably agreed with its philosophy to begin with, and who was in no position to give anything but cooperation to the majority. Yet, at the time of our study, the superintendent could barely light his own cigarette at board meetings, and it was reported that he had begun to develop evidence of ulcers, so tenuous is the position of being "in."

In interviews with the community leaders reportedly in control of each faction, the general admission of a factional structure was made explicit on both sides, by frequent references to "we" and "they," by accusations of clandestine meetings on the part of the other faction, and admitting to getting together for informal talks with one's own faction. Even the specific places, time, and subjects of such meetings were readily admitted on both sides.

An analysis of the votes in a factional board will not convey the true spirit of factionalism unless the analysis is done very carefully, mainly because most of the votes are on issues about which there is little room for disagreement, such as the handling of items of expenditure which, in the factional community, is often voted on individually. If they can, the factional board members avoid a permanent record of their obstreperous behavior. If it comes to voting with the faction or losing an issue, there is no question as to how the vote will fall, although there are instances of faction members not so strongly entrenched as to prevent switching votes on occasion. This occurred on one board meeting which we observed. Two members of the majority had taken the conservative position and two members of the liberal minority had voted against it, with a third member of the liberal minority voting with the two-member conservative majority. This meant that to resolve the matter in favor of the majority, only one of the two remaining conservatives' votes were needed. For about five to ten minutes both members withheld their vote. Both clearly wished the conservative position to be maintained, but neither wished to vote with the conservative majority when it was unnecessary to do so. Eventually, after a long delay, much discussion, and apparent pondering of the issue, both members decided to give in and voted simultaneously with the conservative majority.

Thus, it is clear that an assessment of the board voting patterns may not reveal factionalism for the reason that (1) the large majority of votes are not issues for factional disagreement, and (2) there is a deliberate effort in many cases to avoid the perfect split vote when the factional position can be maintained without straight party-line voting.

Consistent with the proposition that this board was divided along liberal and conservative lines, one would expect report cards to be at issue. In the elementary schools report cards reflected the theory that progress and achievement should be judged in terms of a child's potential. The argument was made that since children's learning rates differ, the most important thing is how he develops as an individual, rather than how he compares with other children. Thus, grades of satisfactory, unsatisfactory, and excellent appeared on the elementary school report card. The conservative majority asked for a revision of the report card on the grounds that it could not tell how well its children were doing. The report card was then brought to the board meeting with slight revisions and the majority sat down and for an hour-and-a-half actually rewrote the report card to represent grades of A through F with a test percentage score represented by each letter. The vote on each of the specific revisions was four to three, with the conservative majority always favoring the revision and the liberal minority opposing it.

Not always were the board meetings so clearly structured around disagreements over issues. There were accusations of favoritism, of obtaining for friends large insurance contracts, of misusing funds for personal expenses, and of personal failings. The executive sessions often ran into the early morning hours. In one case, an assistant principal identified with the liberal minority was a candidate to replace a principal who had been fired. He had already been approved by the community committee recommending the replacement, and by the superintendent's office. The candidate was invited to come to the board meeting, but had to sit out in the hall awaiting approval or rejection for a total of about seventeen hours. At the third meeting, when his appointment was finally taken up, the conservative majority decided it should look elsewhere for a candidate. In all three of the executive sessions, it was reported to us that the minority tried to bring up his name early and clearly indicated that he was waiting in the hall. In the first two sessions, the conservative majority delayed and finally ignored the proposals of the liberal minority. What better evidence do we need that reason becomes puerile in the presence of a majority vote?

THE BASIS OF FACTIONALISM

Conflict at the community level varies in several ways. It may permeate most community decisions or it may be limited to only one institution. We found communities in which there was evident conflict over every issue that came up at the community level, within an organization, or even in informal relations between partisan neighbors. In such communities, we find next door neighbors who will not speak to each other when mowing the lawn and wives who will not talk across the fence or join the same bridge club. Public statements by one person will be contradicted by another, not always because of disagreement over the specific issue but because of long standing identification and enmity.

The basis of such widespread hostility is not always consistent disagreement in the substantive sense. Rather, the fundamental feature of consistent conflict is factional identification. In the community which experiences continued conflict, there are almost always two or three large and powerful factions. Psychological and social identification with these factions is strong. Therefore, when a member of one faction takes a position on some issue, members of an opposing faction must disagree *because of factional membership.*

The identification with the faction becomes all encompassing. The principal criterion in arriving at a decision is the welfare of the faction. The reference group for selecting alternative norms of conduct and belief is the faction. A public figure will avoid taking a position on an issue on which the faction has not yet held a caucus, formal or informal. If asked, the public figure will state, "This needs study."

The faction, as a faction, becomes so important in persistent conflict that we find the "front men" of the faction obtain agreement among themselves on almost every item before it reaches community-wide decision-making bodies. Furthermore, these positions consistently disagree with the positions taken by members of the opposite faction.

In still other communities, we find that only certain issues will bring forth such marked factional identification and cooperation. In one community, a dispute between Protestants and Catholics will bring forth conflict, but items relating to the school will elicit only apathy or the minimum cooperation needed for conducting affairs.

Factional communities do not always exhibit a perfect relationship between obvious splits in the community itself and warring cliques on boards of education. Sometimes, conflicts of interest are institutionalized informally as well. It is common practice in certain communities to insure that representation on boards of education include members from competing interest groups. Depending upon the undercurrents in a particular community, selection is based on the criteria most relevant locally (i.e., town versus gown, labor versus management, ethnic and religious breakdowns, urban versus rural, geographical distinctions, etc.). Irrespective of power components, personality differences may give the impression of factionalism on boards. If the factions are based solely on personality unpleasantries, factions tend to concentrate on petty issues rather than ideological controversies. There may be the appearance of volatility when in reality little overt pressure for change is being exerted on the system. This is not true factionalism.

Because parochial schools still service a large number of students at the elementary and the high school level, religion is a likely arena for serious divisiveness. The fact that religion permeates much of the interaction in many communities creates potentially explosive circumstances which cannot be resolved by ordinary due process mechanisms. The attitudes of factional board members toward each other, if based on religious controversy, run deep, and there is perhaps no basis of factionalism which is more emotionally intense.

Doubtless, there are differences in educational philosophy between at least some parochial schools and the average public school. At the very minimum the systems are competing for the same resources. While differences among the two systems are rapidly disappearing in practice, few parents are aware of it. Moreover, educational disputes that rest on religious grounds may have catastrophic results even though the rhetoric used is out of date by at least one generation.

Two quotations from board members in a large community where the religious factions were unusually antagonistic help to illumine the subtleties involved. These respondents were reporting about the same school system but from an entirely different perspective.

First board member: We have one member whose interest in no way runs along school lines. He sends his children to parochial schools and his real purpose is to undermine and tone down the public schools and make the parochial school system look good in comparison. When he was asked to run, he could not say no. He got his orders from topside.

I think a person has to have guts galore to be a board member and send his kids to a parochial school. The Catholics are a powerful minority and they work underground and indirectly. When a slate of board candidates are listed, people call up my wife to find out which ones are Catholics.

The second board member, referred to previously, had a different conception:

The bishop talked to me about running, and put it on the grounds of discrimination against Catholics. When we hired the new superintendent I had the chancery office check on him. They sent a letter to the parishes where he had been to see what his record had been with Catholics. The approval came back within a week.

Before I leave the board I want a report on how many Catholics have been promoted to administrative positions. We have only one. It doesn't seem reasonable to assume that there aren't some deserving Catholic candidates. Those things are hard to track down. They can say they were considered and were not qualified. That's why we want to get in a position where we can review the candidates for promotion. Then we can assure that Catholics aren't passed over because of religion.

I think it is good to have a Catholic board member. He has no axes to grind. He doesn't have any kids in public school. He can look at things from a point of view that is not prejudiced in any way—no children in school to influence his thinking. I remember a case of a young man who played first string on the local high school basketball team for three years, and he couldn't carry the water bucket for some of the others, but his father was a board member. This gives you an idea of what I mean.

In sum, a minority religious group may, for whatever reason, be charged by the opposition with deliberate self-promoting. As a result, discrimination occurs. The members of the minority group recognize this discrimination and become self-conscious (or more self-conscious). This in itself reinforces and supports the original contention of the majority group, thus creating a vicious cycle between discrimination, reaction to this discrimination, and reinforcement on the basis of the original discrimination. As this self-fulfilling prophecy becomes a reality, the breadth and depth of factional and emotional differences between the two groups greatly intensifies. There is perhaps no basis of conflict which is more difficult to resolve.

In one of our pluralistic communities, we found an entirely different attitude. One Protestant board member put it this way:

> Up until seven years ago there had never been a Catholic member on the board of education. I don't know the origin of putting the first Catholic member on. We have an independent citizens' committee which is made up of people of different religions and different backgrounds who select candidates to run for the school board and I was on that committee. We had one or two members of that committee who objected to having a Catholic on the school board because they supposedly had no interest in the public schools, and really had no right to have any say in the matter. But these people were very understand-

ing when it was explained to them that since Catholics were taxpayers, it was a good idea to have at least one Catholic member.

A Catholic board member in the same community had this opinion:

> Our priest is a pretty liberal and progressive pastor. He never wanted more than one Catholic on the board, and that merely to have representation. He also didn't want a militant Irish Catholic, who says if the Pope says it's so and the pastor says it's so that's what we're going to do. We don't throw our weight around. There have been disagreements, but these have not had anything to do with religion.

These two views of Catholic representation on the board do not differ from the factional community in the sense that the person was there because he was a Catholic. The difference is that each board member takes much the same position, while in the factional community charges and countercharges are commonplace. Again one is impressed with the differences in rhetoric between the various types of communities. In the factional community the Catholic board member talked about protecting the rights of Catholics and eliminating discrimination, while in the pluralistic community the discusson centered around the principle of representation. In the factional community reference was made to checking superintendents in other communities for prejudicial actions against Catholics; in the pluralistic community there was an obvious effort on the part of the Catholics themselves to avoid someone who might be considered dogmatic. In Protestant groups the rhetoric was also quite different—it was a Protestant board member who said that the public school people felt that while Catholics did not send their children to public schools, they were entitled to representation. And most important of all, in one factional community after another we found Protestants saying that Catholics should not be on the board unless they sent their children to public schools. In pluralistic communities we found Protestants arguing that at least one Catholic should be on the board even though he did not send his children to public school.

In most states, political parties do not actively participate in school board elections, but the same kinds of allegiances and attitudes attached to political parties are very much in evidence. Further, in the factional community, the sort of person who is willing to become a candidate for the school board is often the same individual who would run for office for one party or the other. Since it takes planning to get elected to anything, and political parties have the machinery needed for getting out the vote, it would be unlikely that candidates for the board of education would not eventually become party candidates. The following comment, by a board member who later was elected to high political office, is typical of this kind of factionalism:

> *Interviewer:* Why did you decide to run for the school board in the first place?
> *Board Member:* I want to be a judge some day. Nobody ever heard of me except in my own ward. By running for the school board people become familiar with my name. This multiplies one ward by several. I am going to run again for judge. It is a damn frustrating job—this school board. I suppose my ambition to be judge comes first. I really want to be judge.
> *Interviewer:* What about the other board members?
> *Board Member:* This board is mixed up in politics. The

Democratic party nationally set forth the policy of capturing as many local jobs as possible. The Democratic party which is very powerful endorses candidates. One member left our board to be a member of the House of Representatives; another became mayor.

There are states, of course, in which the law provides for representation by political party; in such instances the tendency is to insure that the minority party gets a board member or two. Note the remarks of a school superintendent when asked how his board members were selected:

> He would have to make his desires known to the official people that designate the board members which in this town are the two partisan town committees, the Republican town committee and the Democratic town committee. The town registration is seven to one Republican but under state law there must be minority representation which on a nine man board means three Democrats. The prospective member would make his wishes known to the Republican town committee if he were a Republican and to the Democratic if he were Democratic. Then they would make the decision.

Parties are strong enough to comprise a clear power group. The "conservative-liberal" dimension is frequently too ill-defined and too fluid to comprise a serious analytical pair of factions. When political parties actively participate, a factional board is guaranteed. At the same time professional politicians have learned to work together; competing parties know how to confront each other and there are established rules of the game which encourage a form of stability and insure a relatively disciplined exploration of alternatives.

One community leader in a school district in which a small village had consolidated with a larger city made this statement:

> Have you been to the town of X? They have very few
> people there and cannot possibly offer any kind of good
> educational program for their children. They cannot offer
> two foreign languages, and I'm sure their mathematics is
> not good enough to get into college. But still they fought
> consolidation like mad. I could not understand why they
> were fighting consolidation when it was obvious that there
> was no comparison in what our school could offer their
> children and what their school offers. I suppose it has some-
> thing to do, you know, with identity. Maybe the basket-
> ball team or something like that. But they fought and
> fought to keep their own school.

Small communities often resist consolidation and other types
of centralization even when their children would receive a
better education elsewhere. One of the bases for such resistance was that mentioned by the respondent quoted previously, namely, identification with the school as a symbol of
community pride. Another consideration is the ancient folk
doctrine concerning the evils of urban life. This rationale
may apply even to a very small city when it is proposed
that it consolidate with another small homogeneous community. The antagonisms involved in consolidation become
manifest in many concrete issues of school policy. For example, the need for agricultural education courses, expenditures for life adjustment courses, and extra services defined as
frills by the smaller community may be hotly debated.

    If consolidation does occur, the community members
and board representatives usually find a basis for factionalism
to the degree that they identify with either of the two communities. The following quotation from one of our interviews with a board member from a small community recently
consolidated with a small city is instructive:

Respondent: I served for a long time, about five terms, I believe, on the old board of education. I am running again this time upon the suggestion of a group of farmers.

Interviewer: Were these farmers from your community?

Respondent: Yes. They were mostly friends of mine who I guess like the way our school used to run.

Interviewer: Do you think the present consolidated school board is more liberal than yours used to be?

Respondent: I don't think the liberals are all that liberal but I guess that's what they want to be called. I would say that I am a conservative, but I realize that it takes money to have good schools. So I don't think we have such extreme positions, but I do feel that our smaller school system provided more opportunities for our students. The students from the city get most of the advantages now. It is pretty hard for our kids to break into their cliques.

While the discrimination against farmers is not the same kind that exists against minority groups such as the Negro and the Jew, the words "hick" and "hayseed"—hardly terms of honor and endearment—are often applied to people engaged in agriculture. Such organizations as the Grange drew strength in the beginning by trying to eliminate discrimination of this type. Still, the farmer has fared very well in the smaller rural schools. In fact, agricultural pressures are so powerful in some rural communities that only the official farm viewpoint gets a hearing from the school board.

Even at the college level, the land grant colleges, including experiment stations and the extension services, have received a disproportionate share of tax money and total university effort compared to other occupational groups. This funding is not related to the importance of the occupation itself, but to over-representation in some state legislatures.

Since rural interests usually resist bitterly a takeover by urban centers, if it does happen, rural representatives on boards try to maintain their comparative advantage in any way possible. The result is built-in factionalism.

The interaction between organizational loyalty and educational philosophies is complicated. Doubtless, a board member who represents a faction may sometimes vote against his conscience simply to protect the welfare of the faction. Indeed, the principal criterion for intense conflict in a factional community is the fact that the welfare of the faction outweighs the welfare of the school. However, the political nature of this relationship is not all-consuming inasmuch as membership in a faction is only partly based upon social reasons—employment opportunities, political advancement, peer approval, and the like. Another strong element is cultural; the individual who belongs to a faction subscribes to its tenets in toto.

Therefore, the consistency with which factions vote together is only partly explained by the obvious criterion of self-interest. Most John Birchers accept the party line because it is as compatible with their own preferences, as it is with their views regarding education. One of our boards' members put the matter bluntly:

> You see, these things all fit together. Our idea of education is that the person should learn a lot of facts and have a lot of knowledge. Well, communicating knowledge is simply a matter of having a large classroom, and letting the teacher and the textbook impart this knowledge. You can have a ratio of teachers to students that is fairly economical. With this idea in mind, we can support lower taxes, fewer schools, larger classrooms, and fewer teachers.

The liberals on the board have the idea that the teacher should be in a more one-to-one relationship with each pupil, sort of Mark Hopkins and the log idea. Because of this philosophy, they have to vote for higher taxes, more classrooms, more buildings, and more teachers. You may see us voting as factions on this board, but this split can be based on philosophical grounds just as well as it can on some kind of secret conspiracy.

Those who follow the pluralist persuasion believe that competition among groups tends to produce better community decisions, but they resist the notion that factions stick together across community issues. Our position is that there are communities where conflicts are institutionalized.

In addition to the factions herein explained in detail, other possibilities exist. One of the most visible hard-core factions at the moment is the black population. For years, this group has had little influence on school affairs. Except for the South, blacks have been concentrated in urban areas; the anonymity and detachment of the urban school from black parents has enabled teachers to control the black students within the school building regardless of the size of the school or its locale. Today we find blacks on school boards and we find them advocating community *control* of schools, by which they mean having operating authority, not decentralization under the aegis of a central office bureaucracy. Certainly the specter of race affects almost all community issues in factional communities.

Ethnicity may become as salient a force for factionalism as religion. The Irish name in Boston, the German name in Milwaukee, the Scandinavian name in Minnesota, and the Jewish name in New York City sensitize the voter to certain cultural expectations. It was apparent as we went from community to community that ethnicity did make a difference in the factional community. An Italian-American member of a school board in a pluralistic community is not there to represent his ethnicity; he has been chosen for other qualities. In the factional community his ethnicity may be the reason he was elected to office.

In these days of high property taxes it is not unusual to find a taxpayer's association; such a faction relates itself to all community projects involving tax increases. Resistance to higher costs for education will continue to be encountered, particularly when the increased costs show no measurable improvement in a student's achievement. The public has begun to realize that more money is not by itself likely to produce radical differences in student achievement. The true leadership of a taxpayer's association is likely to be a carefully guarded secret; those who publicly support the organization are generally unknown. Frequently these groups are able to marshal the "silent majority" and defeat community-wide issues. Often their success comes as a big surprise to more liberal supporters of community growth such as the League of Women Voters.

The town versus gown breakdown creates solid cleavages in many college towns, particularly those of comparable size. Professors are demeaned by the hoi polloi of the town as over-educated and ivory towered while professors decry the limited vision of the rest of the population. Student rebellions have tended to exacerbate the situation; the average citizen in the college town is not sympathetic to these expressive outbursts.

THE FACTIONAL BOARD:
A SUMMARY

A factional board is a split board where all major decisions are destined to be decided by the group which can muster a majority vote. Under these circumstances the highly visible role of the board chairman assumes monumental proportions. By using the weapon of parliamentary procedure judiciously he can cut off debate at an advantageous moment, recognize the order of speakers, rule on motions, and generally control the proceedings. Common practice prescribes that the board president and the superintendent of schools jointly develop the agenda for each meeting; a responsibility that enables a determined chairman to significantly influence the sequence in which items will be brought up. Matters of little import may be introduced early and broad debate encouraged so that the energy of the opposition is wasted on relatively minor topics while key issues are reserved for later when resistance has been lowered. It comes as no surprise that the office of board chairman is hotly contested, sometimes taking several ballots; while members of the same faction want to see one of their members win, they are not always agreed on which one it should be.

One of the canons of school board membership is that no member of the board has any authority as an individual; the board when in session speaks only as a body. Factional school board members ignore this dictum with abandon. No board member is free of the nuisance of phone calls at home and the minor irritation of being buttonholed at formal and informal gatherings. But factional board members are apt to meet in a rump caucus to discuss strategy and they are likely to keep in close touch with community leaders of their own persuasion. The majority faction may, if it wishes, devise new rules and regulations on its own volition; the protests of the minority are brushed aside either directly or indirectly.

Public representatives often attend factional board meetings to harass one side or the other. Time is sometimes set aside in the regular board meetings for public-be-heard sessions, which frequently degenerate into vicious name-calling exercises. Devices used by factions to insure that their formal representatives serve their interests are described in the following interview:

> *Interviewer:* What about interest groups in the community? How do they try to exert influence?
> *Board Member:* If you don't mind, I'd like to rephrase that. You say how do they try to exert influence. I claim that they do, trying to is different. They will show up en masse, they will write letters, they will telephone, they will make speeches, they will quiz individual board members in regular meeting if they can get away with it. They will pass resolutions and send us copies of the same, they will appoint committees, and those committees are supposed to meet with board members to go over their concerns item for item. I'm referring here to the most militant groups, the real diamond-studded ones.

A distinguishing characteristic of the factional board is a state of high friction. To be elected in a factional community it is usually necessary to campaign hard and to accuse your opponents of impure motives. It is no wonder that the typical board meeting is filled with hostile rhetoric; both factions try to outdo the other in dispensing invective. While the press may report the choicest retorts, the average citizen cannot help but have a distorted image of the actual proceedings.

6

THE RHETORIC OF CONFLICT AND THE POLITICAL STRATEGIST

Interviews with members of factional communities display a much more vividly colored and outspoken language than that found in dominated communities. There is more swearing, more frequent denunciations of the opposition, more unfriendly remarks, and heavy reliance on strong verbs. Even idle questions, those intended to "warm-up" the interviewee, are reacted to pointedly:

> *Question:* What is there about service on the board of education which gives you the greatest kick?
> *Answer:* That's a hell of a question.

And later, the same interview:

> *Question:* From your experience what would you say is the primary reason most people decide to become board members?
> *Answer:* Damned if I know.

Virile language is expressive of the emotional intensity

of the factional community. In dominated communities labor unions were more inclined to be interested in good education, while in the factional communities labor had a personal stake in controlling the board of education. In the dominated community, businessmen were willing to devote their time to abstract educational policy-making, while in the factional community businessmen tried to capture as much power over the schools as they could. On the dominated board, Mr. Jones may say quietly that he sometimes disagrees with Mr. Smith; on the factional board, Mr. Jones is more apt to say: "Mr. Smith is an absolute idiot, and you can quote me on that."

The flavor of debate—not simply its existence—distinguishes the factional from the pluralistic community. Let us listen to a particularly forceful factional board member:

> I ran on an anti-administration platform. There was a hell of a lot of clean-up work to be done. Before we got the present superintendent, the way teachers were treated was terrible. They were framed on charges of homosexuality and drunkenness. My husband was framed but he got off. I am still trying to get the bastard who did it, but he has walked the chalk line. I'll do it yet though. My first campaign was a bathroom one. Teachers couldn't go to the bathroom between 8:00 and 12:00. One principal made a statement that teachers want to do everything on company time. I told them that at all my speeches and it was very effective. In my early period, every teacher was scared to death.

The hard feelings towards someone which may arise in the heat of debate become permanent memories for factional community members. In the pluralistic community personal recriminations subside when previous protagonists find themselves on the same side in a different set of circumstances.

Both the dominated and pluralistic communities exhibit much less direct mention of power, self-interest, and hyperbole to prove a point. The individuals taking part in the leadership of dominated and pluralistic communities are interested in the issues, active, and attempting to find rational solutions. In the factional community, leaders on an equivalent level are "looking out for their interests, looking out for themselves, and ironing out differences in committee so that they know how the majority vote is going to go."

Ironing out differences in committee is not identical with the consensus model:

> *Question:* If you have difficulty in reaching agreement on issues, how are these differences ironed out?
> *Answer:* Differences would be ironed out in committee. It is rather seldom that you get an issue on the floor. The assistant superintendent got his job on a split vote. At the last meeting of the year the superintendent recommended his appointment. He felt he had control of the board. Many teachers contacted members of the board and expressed dissatisfaction with the proposed assistant superintendent. He is noted as a tyrant. For those reasons it got to be a real issue. You will find splits on driver education. On the subject of giving Blue Cross and Blue Shield to the teachers, two or three did not want to go along with the whole package. On the abolishing of the four-year kindergarten, we had quite an issue, but it ended up as a compromise. What I am trying to say, you can always count on a majority to do one thing or another. You know that before you start.

In other words, compromise means obtaining more than four votes on a seven-man board. Four out of seven votes constitute majority, and the community, the board, and the school personnel are accustomed to such votes. The ready acceptance of such small majorities contrasts sharply with other communities where a prospective close vote might delay decision lest someone say, "With such a small majority why did you go ahead?"

Several factors operate to keep the minority faction self-conscious of its position. In the first place, as one board member put it, getting elected to the board is "hard work." The election campaign appeals directly to prejudices; there is little effort to talk to groups about the broader issues of education. Second, to be elected, an "endorsement" is needed from one of the factional organizations, and these endorsements are not easily forgotten. The board member is expected later to fulfill his obligation to the endorsing agency. Since self-conscious minority factions are unlikely to approve someone ideologically inconsistent with their own beliefs, should a person temporarily erase these obligations from his mind in the process of arriving at decisions, he is sure to be reminded of his transgression.

For instance, newspapers in factional communities closely monitor what is going on behind the scenes, a surveillance which helps keep factional board members honest. Newspapers influence the question of whether boards should enter into private executive sessions. In one large city both newspapers tried to elect candidates, and gave much publicity to the background of each candidate. In this same city the ever-present reporters seemed to inhibit the ability of the board to conduct business in private:

> *Question:* Are there any particular issues you would be reluctant to bring up before the board?
> *Answer:* Yes, we never bring up personal matters. The only things we handle behind the scenes are firing per-

sonnel. There is no time when the press is not present. We frequently don't mention personalities because we are always talking for the record. I disapproved of one of the superintendent's recommendations because the guy was highly dictatorial. At roll call, I got up and said, "I'm going to vote 'no' and it is personal." He went in on a close vote. I shocked people; it was front page. I thought he might sue me for a time.

It is arguable whether newspapers are ultimately responsible for the development of factionalism or whether they just become more interested in school affairs when the drama of factional disputes is present. In any event it is safe to state that given a factional board, the newspaper can and does act to perpetuate the factionalism.

Any superintendent who survives his so-called honeymoon period is by definition minimally successful; therefore, to some degree at least he has mastered the arts of the political strategist. Even the most quiescent school district has nettlesome issues. For instance, some parents may complain about the poor quality of the annual commencement speaker while others are dissatisfied with the performance of the band director. If simple episodes of this magnitude are mishandled consistently, the reputation of the superintendent is destined to become gradually eroded. In short, adopting some of the skills of the political strategists is undeniably part and parcel of being a superintendent. All of this points to an important conclusion: factional school communities and their school boards are engulfed in emotional turbulence, divided loyalties, and incipient bitterness. They are in dire need of highly imaginative and flexible school superintendents.

In factional situations the political strategist role must

be played constantly and consciously. Appeals to idealized norms have very little prospect for success. The options are clear for those who fail to respond. The administrator will decide to opt out because the game is not worth the candle or, more likely, he will be forced to leave involuntarily. We are simply saying that one part of administrative survival is a continuous process of adaptation to complicated social, economic, and technological changes which inevitably take place.

Let there be no misunderstanding. Managing a school system today is no longer a lark. Bond elections, court cases on integration, student uprisings, the constant battle for finances, teachers' strikes, black demands, and the like, all serve to etch furrows on the brow of the most dedicated administrator. Newspapers are often hostile to visible status leaders, not necessarily out of conviction or pique, but due to the inevitable pressure for headlines.

On the subject of "managed news," the Ithaca, New York, *Town Crier* (issue of June 9, 1969), sadly reports the poignant remarks of the ex-president of Cornell University, Dr. James Perkins:

> In our preoccupation with campus peace security, there is no question that we failed to anticipate the impact of the series of photographs that were taken as the students left Willard Straight Hall. If the black students could have been persuaded to leave quietly by bus, as we urged them to do, the public reaction to this episode would have been a small fraction of what it actually was. We have learned that the news media in America exacts a high price from those who neglect the tremendous impact of photographic shorthand that is not sufficiently and carefully explained to the public.

Philosophers from Plato to Karl Jaspers have engaged in serious disputations concerning the merits of the statesman versus the politician. "I would rather be right than be President" epitomizes the suspicion held by many in the body politic that no bureaucratic official can continuously maintain integrity in the face of the multiple pressures applied to him. Many of these purists will say that school administration should exist apart from politics because they believe that the job is simply a matter of technique. If by integrity is meant that the school administrator must always have his way in the de Gaulle manner, then, of course, we have few statesmen in educational politics. Local school systems are entirely too responsive to the people to permit an appointed official this measure of autocratic authority. No superintendent speaks ex cathedra in a factional community unless he has decided that his job is no longer worth the effort required to satisfy the expectations of a diverse constituency.

School systems are fairly open in terms of political access. Like state legislatures, their business is conducted in public, and parliamentary stratagems and polarized argumentation become routinized and acceptable. Board meetings may break into bitter debates often inflamed by the presence of radicalized groups representing particular points of view. The superintendent who finds himself enmeshed in this cauldron of competing interests is required to remain relatively free of personal identification with the various factions in order that he may be perceived as impartial enough to seek a working compromise. It is not likely that any special interest group will get everything it wants; if it should, temporary gains may quickly be erased at the next board election.

There are men in public life able to place themselves

above politics, who influence the minds of the powerful without engaging in the effort and organization needed to achieve grass-roots support. Such advisors who avoid the nitty-gritty of political work are free to escape their institutional responsibilities when their advice turns sour, not so the captive school administrator. The school superintendent must pay the price for his office, and he feels the pain when matters go awry. Skill, merit, conciliatory behavior, and consistency are marks of his trade; he cannot fall back on aristocratic background and powerful friends in time of trouble, for in most cases he is the product of a lower middle-class background and he must depend upon his own resources almost exclusively.

There is little doubt that boards of education in high-conflict districts influence the work of the superintendent. Take the case of Big City as a prime example.

Big City is a large, economically diversified industrial city. Its board members run for six-year terms in a city-wide election. Candidates are nominated at a non-partisan primary election; general election runoffs determine the winners. As many as forty candidates may offer themselves in the primary election. In the event there is a vacancy between elections the board appoints a replacement. To run as an incumbent definitely benefits a candidate.

The board is an independent taxing unit; hence the president of the board ranks next to the president of the city council in the city government structure.

In order to be elected in this city it is necessary to engage in active grass-roots politics; no caucus or inside group is able to control the selection process. For this reason candidates with practical political skill hold a strategic advantage. The quotation below illustrates a typical campaign technique:

> Running for election is really grim. You have to be a good sport. You must be willing to go all out. You must work like everything. You have to do it yourself, endorsement is not enough. A great many people who are good do not run just because of the running itself. The appointment system has its drawbacks too. You have to know the back-room of every saloon in town. I made three to four meetings a night for three months. Of course, running successfully has nothing whatever to do with being on the board.

Endorsement by labor seems to be of inestimable value to a candidate. Note the comments by a board member who won without labor backing:

> You see labor has a real stake in the board election. The building trades are involved because of our building contracts. The teacher's union is interested in salaries. Labor endorses its candidates. Prior to the election a little card is printed which contains all the names of their endorsed candidates. The card is distributed by the shop stewards at the factory. It is a very powerful way of campaigning. The statement has been made that ninety percent of the homes in the city are reached in this way because everything is so completely unionized.

The attitude of a board member who received labor support offers a contrary point of view:

> I was interviewed by labor. The only commitment they exacted from me was that I keep a free and open mind. I received their endorsement. When labor gave me their endorsement I was a cinch. It wasn't even close. We are

accused of not being independent. I feel absolutely independent. Labor only asks that I do not sneer at their proposals.

Oddly enough, it is still possible for a board member to be elected without extensive campaigning or labor support; however, he must have a name which is well known or respected in the city, as shown by comments such as these:

> My name is synonymous with education. There was a fellow with my name who was superintendent of schools for thirty years. One of my colleagues gets in the same way. He is not labor endorsed and he is very conservative but the people vote the name. I know that I will be re-elected so I don't give a damn what the rest of the board thinks.

> I can stay on the board forever due to my name and the support of the Catholic church.

It is the ballot box, pure and simple, which sorts out the candidates. The only standard which all must meet is political acumen. The statement below by a member with twenty years' service on the board summarizes the election procedures neatly:

> It may be one of the weaknesses of the American way of life that everyone is entitled to run. The opportunity is available to any individual. All you need is one percent of the last vote for governor as signatures. Our newspaper carries a complete biography of each candidate. If any voter cares to he can look this up. Human nature is funny. People will vote for names that are sound. Also they vote on religion—which ones are Catholics and which are non-Catholic. There is no excuse for the citizenry not being aware. There is a pendulum swinging toward labor

—labor is getting the upper hand. Labor issues invitations for candidates to come down. They cross-examine you. They ask general questions and shoot some hypothetical questions. Labor sponsors an all union slate. Of course, some people don't vote as the union says or as the priest tells them. In the ballot box you are still a free agent.

Much of the board work is done in standing committees. Each board member is assigned to one major committee by the board president. These committees play a very active role and their recommendations to the board proper have considerable influence in decision making. The press is present at committee hearings as well as the official board meeting. Note how issues are generally resolved:

> The issues are assigned to the proper committee. We have five members on committees. We think through the thing and discuss it pro and con. We generally come to some understanding in committee. Of course the total board has the final say but in the interest of harmony most of the committee recommendations are accepted. They have the time to study and evaluate the problem. They can call individuals in for a hearing and get the necessary information.

There is considerable disunity on the board. Minority members often choose a relatively simple issue, such as the appointment of the board representative to the public library board, to precipitate a contest. It has taken as many as forty ballots to elect the board president due to the power which accrues to this position; the president of the board becomes chairman of the strategic committee in control of staff appointments.

The members do not owe allegiance to each other and

they do not hesitate to decide issues by majority vote. Feuds may develop over different viewpoints but generally the quarrels are related to status prerogatives such as election to board president and the like. The quotations below indicate how controversial problems are decided:

> Differences are never ironed out. Many times it comes down to a vote and by a majority, that's it. You can follow your convictions this way.
>
> Differences are decided by the sheer power of votes. That's it, that's the truth.

The board is an embattled band in more ways than one. Some members support the superintendent avidly; others make bitter and disparaging remarks about his ability. They do not appear to like each other; there is no group solidarity. The following series of quotations illustrate this lack of consensus:

> I am quite a bit disturbed with the relationship a board member can have with the superintendent. Personal contacts seem to put fear in our superintendent. There is a certain amount of disrespect connected with the size of the board and the kind of people serving on it. You can be hurt by personality assassination. Our superintendent is a prodigious worker but he lacks several things. Quite frankly I have esteem for not more than three colleagues of mine. Politics and religion have nothing to do with this.
>
> Not more than five of our board carry the ball or have the background and ability to do so. The others pretty much sit and vote. It is a nice pleasant job. They don't participate in the discussions, they are nonentities. Board members ought to be more vigorous. Some are vigorous on a

most adverse side. They are always thinking up ways to embarrass the superintendent. If they were vigorously critical, they would be a real help.

I get annoyed when you have to work with board people with an area of interest even though they know it would upset statutes. People who are purely labor and ask questions like 'Did union help do this?' Also the group which is purely parochial school oriented and have no pattern for public schools. There is a lot of bitterness connected with this issue. I have been to Europe so I know what can happen in a dominated country.

On the board we have a clique which was supported by the non-partisan group. You can't tell whether they are fish or fowl. In the ward where I was strongest in the primary they had the colored handing out cards like mad against me. There is some danger to the community in this. It produces schisms and splits on the board. I don't like what I smell. Fortunately it is a weakening group and labor has the greatest strength.

Any recommendation of the superintendent may become the focus for board conflict; even a personnel appointment has been known to result in a hairline vote. One member expressed the situation aptly when he asserted "you can always trust a majority of people to do something."

The political cast in Big City is so apparent and well publicized by the mass media that educational debates are liberally laced with partisan outcomes. The superintendent's tenure is subject to the whims and fancies of a bitterly split board of education. He is tolerated, respected for his technical understanding of the educational process, but he is not loved or admired. Should he attempt to suggest a course of action which would endanger the political future of any board member, the votes will just not be there. Naturally, he is too smart to precipitate a conflict which he cannot win; administrators who are masochistic enough to challenge a system of this type without adequate backing are doomed to failure.

For all its obvious faults, the factional community represents in reality the closest approximation to the democratic process of any of our ideal types. The decisions may not fit the preferred solutions of experts, but they do represent what the people think they want. The administrator who works in Big City has to learn to take the important issues to the people if he wishes to get results. If he can attract the attention of the general citizenry by his pronouncements, he has the opportunity to make substantive changes. The very openness of board decision-making makes it difficult for the board to dismiss a popular leader without sufficient cause. If his popularity wanes due to setbacks (deserved or undeserved), the board will be quick to unseat him. It is always dangerous to aim for big stakes, but then if you don't like to take chances it is wiser not to become a superintendent in strife-ridden districts.

Debate as to which group—students, faculty, board of education, citizens, or administration—should run the public schools has never reached the crescendo universities have had to face. Local control of schools has meant that the local school board exercised great independence in determining curriculum, selecting teachers, and generally controlling the schools, while individual teachers and students participate little in these decisions. Signs on the horizon portend a change in this comfortable arrangement.

Still, the *Chicago Tribune* gleefully reported the ousting

of the Evanston elementary school superintendent by a four to three vote. (Its own reporter was a member of the school board.) The editorial comments of this influential newspaper make interesting reading:

> Like the former school superintendent in Chicago, Benjamin C. Willis, Dr. Coffin has a reputation for arrogance, abrasiveness, and unwillingness to communicate sufficiently with the board. This was cited in the confidential letter the board made public early yesterday morning after the vote against retaining its superintendent. Like Willis, Coffin also has excellent credentials as an educator. His weakness is that he tries sometimes to dictate programs rather than sell them.[1]

Dr. Coffin is reputed to have identified the key issue for his dismissal as a dispute between "liberals versus conservatives." The *Tribune* reported that Dr. Coffin stated he had done to the best of his ability everything asked for, to the point of being so polite and humble that he did not even speak up when he felt it difficult to restrain himself. Bonapartism clearly does not work in the public school setting if there are disagreements about goals and priorities. Once a school board becomes highly politicized, it finds it impossible to establish some kind of consensus about what should be done, say, in the event of a student strike. The superintendent becomes expendable because he is essentially a target around which hostility can focus. Like faculties in universities, public school faculties, accustomed to virtual immunity from outside interference (most are tenured with full job security), are particularly inept at dealing with political pressures generated by people who do not subscribe to judicial bargaining but instead choose the route of naked power. Superintendent

Coffin had the unanimous support of his sub-administrative group; it went for naught.

School politics is a mercurial process, a fact well known to the political strategist. The existence of strong competitive factions in school political circles has been documented repeatedly.[2]

The Levittown school board is a classic case and fits our model perfectly. There were essentially two groups in Levittown vying for power; on one side was the Better Education League and on the other was the Information and Education Committee. The support for each group was so evenly divided in the community that each election might see one group triumph over the other. The campaigns resembled a gutter brawl with accusations and counter-accusations filling the columns of the local Long Island newspapers. The upshot was a split board. The superintendent tended to lean toward the Better Education League point of view (this group appeared to be willing to spend more money for education) and when the Information and Education Committee gained control of the board, the superintendent was fired unceremoniously. While much fanfare occurred including an investigation by the NEA and the State Education Department, harassment of the new superintendent continued. By harassment, we mean petty requests for information, deferring of action on important issues, open repudiation of ideas in public meeting, and internal bickering on inconsequential matters.

Divisive communities require a superintendent who is psychologically constituted to withstand a great deal of ambiguity. Under the threat of instant dismissal should he incur the ire of the majority in control of the board, he must progress slowly. These factional cases we have been describing are much more common than is generally realized; under most circumstances an effort is made to keep these internal feuds from bursting into public view.

There are several ways in which a superintendent can work with the majority of his board and still not offend the minority. One manner is to give the appearance of working hard on behalf of both sides. In one community, factions were split between a highly organized but small Kiwanis Club and a disorganized but numerically larger Catholic population. Voting superiority enabled the Catholic faction to maintain control of the school board. The superintendent had held his position for a long time and he was well liked by both factions. It was apparent that while he went along with the Catholics most of the time, he protected himself by laboring for the minority. As one respondent put it: "Our superintendent is a member of our Kiwanis Club and he's a pretty hard working member of it too."

Factions may balance themselves fairly evenly. Therefore, the superintendent must maintain some relationship with both factions if he is to maintain his job when the minority faction of this year becomes the majority faction of next year. But, if he is to get anything done, he must work with the majority. Such a tight wire is the major feature of the life style of the superintendent in a factional situation.

A ready mechanism which permits the superintendent a little running room is the ancient bureaucratic ploy of silence. Firm statements, even when they appear to be innocent at the time, may lead to later difficulties. For instance, the projection of school population, a fairly simple procedure which is usually non-controversial, can erupt into a bitter issue.

The superintendent in a conflict environment is well advised to refrain from direct statements even on matters of fact.

A quotation given by one of the leaders in a factional community, in this case a minority faction, clearly indicates part of the reason a superintendent in a factional situation benefits from general rather than specific pronouncements:

> *Respondent:* The state law regarding libraries is absurd. Now understand me, I am all for reading books. However, we have a lot of troubles other than libraries in this community. Our home economics department is ridiculous. It does not have any facilities at all. On the other hand, we have three libraries and there are many books in the public library that the children have not read. I went to the superintendent on three different occasions and talked to him about this. I asked him what the state law said on library use and I could never get a clear answer from him. He just kept talking and saying things. I guess there are certain things they can spend that money for and certain things they cannot, is that right? I guess they thought maybe they could spend that money for real troubles in our school, but later on found out that they could not. I guess they can't turn down the money because it does mean a better school library although we do not need it. I just couldn't get anything out of the superintendent which told me exactly how the money could be spent, what it was intended for, or whether it could be used to build up our home economics program.

On the factional board, the necessity for the superintendent to be coy about wholehearted support of majority decisions is a safety measure he cannot afford to overlook, although it often annoys the majority. In one factional community where the superintendent has been in office for about twenty years, the leading conservative of the board was asked

whether or not there was any difficulty between the board
and the administration:

> *Respondent:* This is confidential isn't it? We sometimes
> have an occasional disagreement, although it's not very
> obvious. It is just that the administrator fails to carry
> through on something we vote. He often forgets how the
> vote went. He sometimes gets interested in some other
> program and forgets.
>
> *Interviewer:* Could you give me a specific example?
>
> *Respondent:* Well you're sure this is confidential? I
> wouldn't want to put anybody on a spot. For example if a
> teacher might do a certain thing which we disapproved and
> the superintendent thought was OK, he might be a little
> forgetful that we had decided to clamp down on her. Maybe
> that's the wrong word to use. But you know what I mean.

The hiring of teachers is usually a professional matter,
and the criteria are formally set by the board upon the advice
of the superintendent. In most states, each teacher is approved
by the board after being hired by the superintendent. On occasion, the political philosophy of a teacher is questioned.
In the factional community this becomes a most sensitive
issue, and the careful superintendent plays his role differently
than he would in another type of power structure. On this
issue, one conservative member of a factional board said:

> *Respondent:* Well take for example the hiring of a
> teacher. I remember recently that a fellow was hired from a
> teacher's college who had been pretty active in campus
> politics. Reports got to the superintendent that he had also
> run around with some pretty unsavory friends during his
> college days. Now in a case like this the superintendent will
> check with some of us. I don't know whether he checks
> with all the board members or not, but I know he checks
> informally with me.

> *Interviewer:* Would the superintendent just talk to the majority members of the board?
> *Respondent:* No, the superintendent would talk to the officers of the board.

The officers on this board were elected on the basis of seniority and could be reelected. The board's majority members represented the long-standing population of the community; the minority on the board represented those who had migrated to the community more recently. Consequently, the officers of the board were from the conservative majority. How the superintendent would react if a minority member were to become chairman is unknown, and an unlikely event.

The democratic process is based on the assumption that there are important differences of opinion which deserve discussion if a fair compromise is to be effected. What does one do when groups of persons are obdurate in their differences of opinion? What, especially, does one do when these groups hold the possibilities of one's future achievement and success in their hands? The answer is to turn to the committee, the mechanism of democratic consensus-building.

The intense differences present in factional communities may frequently lead to the exploitation of democratic mechanisms for pure protection against reprisals. One politically-minded superintendent was described by an interviewer in the following way:

> This superintendent would, when an issue came up, appoint committees to study the issue—unwieldy committees of 100 people. If there were two alternatives, he would appoint two committees of 100 people each. He completely floored the board members with research, minutes of past meetings, orientation schedules, and completely bogged down the board members—keeping them off bal-

ance. Each board member had stacks of research reports at least 18 inches high—literally. They couldn't read all of it, so they had little to attack the superintendent on.

Superintendents who find themselves in communities where school government is blatantly political have special handicaps to overcome. Our research experience has led us to conclude that these high-friction school districts generally attract relatively young and aggressive board members, who strongly represent ethnic or religious groups holding non-prestigious occupational roles, and are more supportive of vocational than intellectual education. In a typical situation, the superintendent is usually older, more informed and experienced with regard to educational matters, but hamstrung by the environmental constraints under which he is forced to work.

One industrial suburb of a large city well illustrates this trend. The board members interviewed had not yet achieved any marked success in their own occupations and looked upon membership on the school board as a stepping stone to political and economic success. None of the members had any experience in management roles and their decisions reflected this lack of understanding. Here is what the board president told us:

> There was almost a teacher's strike before I got on the board and the schools were in a mess. The old board hired all the teachers and the teachers were revolting about everything. The superintendent didn't have anything to do about hiring the teachers—they had to go through the board. This went all the way through the janitorial staff. In fact if you wanted to be a janitor the practice was to see a board member, get his approval, and then you might get the job.

In his opinion it was incorrect for the board members to get involved in the nitty-gritty of selecting teachers but he had a different idea about custodians:

> I can't see where it does any harm to let school board members select the janitors. This is the only way you can return favors for friends who have helped you get elected. In fact I can't see any harm in it at all as long as the favor is related just to the hiring. Once the man gets into the job then it's his responsibility to keep his nose clean. I can't see where the janitors affect the educational process anyway.

Prescriptions for proper behavior have been written and enshrined in codes for superintendent–administration–board relationships in practically every state of the union, but these trite statements are weak reeds indeed if there is an absence of trust between the superintendent and the board. Any superintendent worth his salt will not debase himself beyond a certain point; this critical juncture varies with the individual and the circumstance. No superintendent likes to be ceremoniously dismissed; such an action is strongly symbolic of failure. The superintendent may have made no errors in judgment, his decision to withdraw from his position may have been courageous and necessary, but there lingers behind the inevitable undercurrent that somehow this man failed to meet the challenge. It is small wonder that the superintendency has been labeled the "uneasy profession."

NOTES

1. *Chicago Tribune,* June 25, 1969.
2. Joseph F. Malone, "The Lonesome Train in Levittown," *The Inter-University Case Program,* rev. ed., Tuscaloosa, Alabama: University of Alabama Press, 1958.

PART FOUR

THE PLURALISTIC COMMUNITY, THE STATUS CONGRUENT BOARD, AND THE SUPERINTENDENT AS PROFESSIONAL ADVISOR

In some communities there are many active interest groups, well organized to exert influence on school issues but not sufficiently large to wield power alone. The chief resource of such groups is primarily manpower (or more likely woman-power). The key difference between this type of pluralistic community and the factional community is the constant re-alignment of groups siding together on issues.

The ability of these groups to combine temporarily to influence policy forces school board members to pay constant attention to community sentiment. Equally important, these temporary alignments often recruit candidates for school board membership. The board members debate issues and this debate often changes votes. It is important to delineate the pros and cons if the board is to avoid major crystallization of opposition among the various groups. A board member's status, therefore, is not determined by his position in a single power structure nor by his rank in one faction or another, but rather is congruent with his ability to articulate a position.

Clearly, what is needed by such a board is someone who has a professional understanding of education to serve as consultant—such is the textbook version of the superintendent's role: the professional advisor.

7

DEBATES AND
SHIFTING
ALLIANCES

The theory of conflict states that if it is expressed in situations where people hold essentially the same values as to ends, and if competing organizations allow for open conflict to solve problems—in other words, if they institutionalize the conflict—then the expression of conflict itself performs many of the functions of divergent groups and their members. By allowing groups to identify problem areas and antagonistic feelings which may be affecting a small minority, solutions may be negotiated with the full participation of those who stand to lose by the results. Through the close associations developed in these exchanges and newly formed coalitions, a cohesiveness may develop which is beneficial to the community's social structure. Still other positive results may occur through the acting out of conflicts, but this does not mean it will help all situations. For instance, conflicts in which individuals and groups do not share basic values threaten to disrupt the social structure and develop into permanent factions.

In the pluralistic community, the tolerance of conflict which exists is the very means by which better decisions are reached; the confrontations that emerge do not tear the community apart.

There is a surprising air of awareness on the part of citizens in the pluralistic community toward the positive functions of conflict and confrontation, whereas the popular image of conflict portrays it as inherently wicked. Observe how a female community leader reacted to a committee meeting she attended: "They avoided the issue rather than confront each other." This realistic appraisal boldly rejects non-risk-taking behavior.

Naturally, the tone of each confrontation is extremely important. Later on in the interview this same respondent said:

> We have a small community and we all know each other and even when there are differences of opinion it's all very polite and courteous. The conduct of board meetings is very calm and casual. The board members don't scream and shout at each other. They do debate issues aggressively; however, I've never seen a board meeting with people really upset. The board members are smart enough to see the community as it is, not as one might like it to be.

From the point of view of the dissemination of information alone, it is unfortunate that the word "conflict" is often considered to be dysfunctional in the decision-making process. Open hearings held to entertain an honest confrontation of ideas in a courteous atmosphere have the often unappreciated advantage that the protagonists do not have to personalize their differences.

The outstanding feature of the pluralistic community is the presence of ever-shifting alliances. In these realignments, the emotionally tinged memory of past "enemies" is softened by teamwork with that past "enemy" in another arena of activity. The pluralistic community seems to sense that conflict and creativity may well go together.

Frequently we find pluralistic communities existing in suburban communities where peoples' values and life styles are similar. In our opinion Dahl's pioneer study of pluralistic but blighted New Haven is somewhat of a special case. Most industrial cities tend to fall in the factional category. In order not to fall into stereotypes we have selected as our case study a community that had once been dominated by one very large industry. The city itself is small to medium in size, but its major industry has been affiliated with one of the leading corporations in the United States.

This industry has been based on the presence of plentiful natural resources, and when these resources became severely depleted, the industry collapsed. The industry's powerful domination of the community, admitted by everyone interviewed, had disappeared something less than a decade ago. The result was that many groups, almost all of which had been concerned about the schools during the period of domination but saw no outlet for their opinions, assumed leadership in the vacuum left by the rapid disappearance of the dominant single industry. The groups most interested in the public schools were an organized band of Catholics, two leading Protestant churches, a labor union, the Chamber of Commerce, and an active PTA organization. At various times other interests came to the front over a particular issue, but generally they were not active. The standard of living in the community was relatively low, at least by national standards. There was a fairly thriving middle class, a working class that had difficulty in getting jobs and maintaining economic security, and a lower class which eked out a living or was on welfare.

Prior to our entrance in the community a controversy had come up. On the one side were the Catholics, the labor union, and the Chamber of Commerce; on the other were the two Protestant churches, the PTA, and another organization which ordinarily did not involve itself in school affairs. A tax bond referendum, which the former were against and the latter for, had failed. Those advocating passage of the bond issue were loosely organized and their campaign was fairly mild-mannered; most of the voters for the bond issue could not see how it could possibly fail and consequently stayed away from the polls.

Another issue came up in which one of the leading citizens, a woman member of the PTA, was asked to chair a committee to revise the elementary report card. She met with some of the PTA members informally, and they decided that report cards for the elementary schools should be changed from a strict grading of mastery of subject matter to a reflection of the relationship between progress and potential. At this time, she asked that a community-wide committee be formed to represent the various elements in the community. She sought out representatives from the Catholic church, from the two Protestant churches, and from the Chamber of Commerce. She also sought but failed to get support from the labor union leadership. In the committee finally appointed, there were people representing organizations which had been aligned against each other on the school bond issue. Nevertheless, the committee worked well as a unit, and recommended a revised and progressive elementary report card which it then submitted to the school superintendent. The committee spent a great deal of time eliciting support from all visible community units. The chairman personally contacted the pastor of the Catholic church; she also spoke to the Chamber of Commerce on the rationale behind the new report card.

When the report card was submitted by the superintendent's office to the school board for approval, an open hearing was held to review the recommendation. Unexpectedly, there was no representation from the labor union, but, also unexpectedly, the Chamber of Commerce opposed the new report card on the grounds (1) that parents would not know how well their children were doing competitively and (2) that employers needed to know a potential employee's record of achievement. It was also mentioned that institutions of higher learning require grades in order to predict how well a student will do in college. The committee chairman countered with the argument that high school grades were sufficient for employers and colleges and universities.

After a lengthy discussion the school board voted to accept the new elementary report card. The key factor in this decision was the new alignment of interest groups. There were no stable factions and no dominating structure controlling school matters. The way to effect change in school policy was to secure an alignment consisting of groups neither for nor against each other, but simply independent of each other.

The superintendent had appeared on radio in support of the bond issue, but he did not speak vehemently. Rather, he spoke in terms of professional concepts: the need for additional classrooms, small teacher-pupil ratios, and the like. To support the new report card he quoted research evidence that elementary students did benefit from a more flexible grading policy. He played the role of the professional advisor and with quite successful results. His quiet but effective support offended no one, and the lady who was the chairman of the committee to introduce the new report card said that he was behaving in the manner she expected. The school board members, when asked about his behavior, said simply that he was performing his job—it was the board's prerogative to decide and the superintendent's responsibility to appoint the committee, present its report to the board with a recommendation, and give the board the understanding it needed to decide on the issue.

Pluralism explicitly rejects the idea that the definition of goals and the means to achieve them should be decided solely by a ruling elite. Likewise, pluralistic communities make certain that there is no single unchecked source of power.

Part of this independence of mind is engendered by the high cultural level of most of these communities. The citizens are more likely to read the *Wall Street Journal* than *Reader's Digest*. (Observations of this type are quickly picked up when you interview people in their homes, which we frequently did.) Their relative affluence and their propensity for travel encourage a more cosmopolitan view of the world. It is commonly recognized by citizens in a pluralistic community that most of the controversial matters faced at the local level cannot be disassociated from national and state concerns. Debate occurs without respite, but the focus of attention is not on whether the local fire station should be repainted or not. A newspaper editor in one of our pluralistic communities summed up the character of people's concern:

> I think that basic antagonisms between a community and its schools develop at a time when the difficulties are national in character. Take the case of McCarthyism. We drew up a sensible policy to take care of that. This happened in 1952 but our policy is still in effect. The same is true on cases of moral and spiritual values which became a very important topic and of great concern to people of this country not too long ago. A district like this is generally out in front in issues of this kind. We anticipate; we do not wait for the axe to fall.
>
> Back in 1958 a few people got upset about Sputnik. They said we're not doing well in our schools so they had a big discussion over our lack of foresight. But strangely enough, this irritation calmed right down rather suddenly. We indicated that we were ahead of Conant and his recommendations. When you get people who are concerned and who will work hard at correcting an inequity, such as we have, you have to be continually 'on the ball.' We have found out, though, that in the long run everything will right itself. Our constituency is just too bright to accept simplistic solutions.

In this circumstance and elsewhere throughout the pluralistic communities studied, we found a broad-minded attitude toward deviant opinions and an accompanying faith that eventually any extremism would be diluted by open public debate. There was certainly no absence of activity on the part of special interest groups in our pluralistic communities; but the determined activism of more moderate groups tended to prevent the growth of identifiable factions.

While it is not necessary for a community to have wealth

for it to be labeled pluralistic, it helps. Funds available to managerial personnel can encourage the maintenance of an active and viable community life without developing the kind of bitter conflict that leads to factionalism. The type of people who have access to assets external to the community are likely to be experienced in the handling of decisions involving very large sums of money, numbers of people, and carrying enormous responsibility. Hence, many issues which might become controversial in less sophisticated climates become simply, in the pluralistic community, matters for rational decision-making based upon the best experience and understanding available. Only a very few at the top have these characteristics in some dominated communities, and often no citizen has such experience.

In a pluralistic environment, once the interest groups most affected have decided upon a course of action the manifold resources of modern management are used to communicate to the public. For instance, in one of our sample communities, the location of a new school had been laboriously determined by an ad hoc committee. The vice-president of the telephone company in the region had been the chairman of the committee which made the decision. He brought in executives from his company with "displays and gadgets and did a wonderful job in presenting the material to the public." In this fashion a favorable vote was assured.

A standard pattern observed in almost every pluralistic community is the heavy reliance on community-wide committees. The committee system stresses the bureaucratic faith in facts and rationality. It is a cooptative technique of incomparable strength. While universal acceptance of committee reports never occurs, a high proportion of them are ratified.

Committees rely on specialized knowledge and fact-finding assignments are made in terms of a person's representing relevant interests. Consequently, the deliberations and conclusions are carefully weighed by decision-making agencies.

This operating pattern has the significant advantage of providing a considerable amount of expertise on committees and insuring that the first step toward organized community support in any field of endeavor is a well-documented committee report.

One characteristic that distinguishes the pluralistic community from others is its all-around excellence in decision-making. There are communities which seem to wallow in a sea of mediocrity, their leaders either disinterested or incompetent. Most of these unfortunate places are depressed urban centers or islands of rural poverty, where local control lacks the talent needed to raise standards to an acceptable level.

A community leader ably summarized the distinguishing features of pluralism in this way:

> If anything we have too many leaders; there are not enough followers. Most of the people in this city feel it is their duty, even at personal sacrifice to their business and home life, to do their part for the community. I know that it has often been said that the bulk of the population is apathetic but you would never know it here. We have a majority who are intellectually active and concerned; no matter what is under consideration you can expect to find all sorts of people willing to get into the act.

The factional community may seem in some of its behavior to approximate the pluralistic type. The most telling factor is not the presence of open, heated exchanges between groups, but whether the factions stay together regardless of the barrenness and divisiveness of the issue at stake. If they do persist to cohere, independent of the issue, then their behavior follows the model of factionalism.

On the whole, pluralistic communities depend more than other communities on a thorough investigation of relevant facts before reaching important decisions. As one respondent stated:

> The individual or group who tries to influence us better be well prepared. We are not impressed with sophistry or oratory. That's why you will find that the same people don't try to sponsor every new program that comes along. It is just too time consuming. Once you have conducted a campaign in favor of one policy you are less likely to continue on to another right away. Anyway there are plenty around who are willing to take up the cudgel and this helps get new blood into action.

Obviously, the way to get things done in a democracy is to pull as many groups as possible together in support of common interests; the pluralistic community generates the capacity to reach this goal.

We asked a board member in one of these "best" communities how he accounted for its vitality. His comments bear remembering:

> I suppose the main thrust is the high quality of individuals who are attracted here. We have first-rate public services, good zoning laws, a superb country club, a fine mix of business and professional men. Their wives are no slouches either. It takes money to live in this community; taxes are high and are getting higher. The people who move into our town do not hesitate to pay a premium for a house. There are no vacant lots around as you can see.

We have zip because every man around is near the top of his own field. Men like that are not stampeded easily; they will support improvements if they can be convinced of the necessity. We don't permit pressure groups to intimidate us. If it is a legal matter we consult some of our own Wall Street lawyers. This works for any field. I don't think you can find a better community than ours.

STATUS CONGRUENT BOARDS: DECISION BY CONSENSUS

One of the main criticisms leveled at boards of education recently is that they are anachronistic and incapable of reforming themselves. The assumption is made that because the administrators possess all the information and expertise, there is no way the board of education can provide an effective check on their operating decisions.

Admittedly, there may be instances in which the above description is reasonably accurate. The status congruent board, however, is quite capable of performing effectively. Ordinarily, its members understand their roles; they do not meddle with or overrule the administration nor do they pry into the internal affairs of the faculty. Yet, they wish to play a significant role in the over-all policy making of the institution or they would not take on these community responsibilities; they are definitely disinterested in rubber stamp activities.

A description of a typical status congruent board may reveal more clearly the ingredients needed. Statusville is one of the finest residential suburban areas in the United States with a population composed almost exclusively of upper-class social and economic groups. Its seven board members are elected for three-year terms by popular vote at a non-partisan spring election. The principle of democratic representation is supposedly maintained by a community caucus that recommends the candidates to the electorate; these candidates usually run unopposed.

All of the school board members represent people of substance in the community: the present board includes a banker, two attorneys, a housewife, a contractor, a retailer, and a public relations executive. These men and women are long-term residents, Republican, economically secure, active participants in community life, and excellent spokesmen for their constituency. Membership cannot be otherwise due to the system of selecting candidates. Note how the selection process operates:

> We have a school board caucus. The caucus system is devised to have representation from all areas of the township. They screen and recommend various candidates put up by each village. Each year when I was president, I met with this committee about future plans and past accomplishments. Each village makes its own recommendations for the board and they are voted on by the public. The caucus is usually it; very seldom a contest. Ballots provide for write-in votes but they are never heavy or significant.

"The office seeks the man" was the recurrent theme used by board members to explain their willingness to serve. Acceptance of board membership becomes a matter of *noblesse oblige* in view of the honor bestowed by this form of selection. An interesting illustration of the criteria used may be found in this quotation: "I think they probably use background and record of participation in community affairs plus personal judgement as to the individual's interest, willingness to work, and intelligence."

Board procedures are designed to encourage debate with the ultimate objective of reaching consensus. The board is completely free of built-in conflict; feuds involving cliques of members are noticeably absent. Disagreements arising over different viewpoints are subjected to group discussion and normally an amicable solution can be reached. Of course, no group is entirely free of stress and members did express contrary opinions, but because the members are true peers and closely identified with each other, a fundamental schism is not apt to occur. Note the specific process employed to settle differences:

> Differences generally are talked out fully. In most cases agreements are reached by kicking pros and cons around. Where agreement is not possible, it will come down to a compromise. When compromise is not forthcoming—say three or four times a year—it is a vote with the majority holding forth. This happens rarely actually.

Controversies on the board are almost always due to differing viewpoints regarding the means to ends accepted by all. Members are agreed on the general purposes of the school system and the caucus method of selection practically guarantees a kind of homogeneity of interest. As one member said: "We don't seem to have any basic differences in our community. Our interests are similar. Once we understand there are very few differences."

Board solidarity of this type does not free the administrator from worry. A highly prestigious board expects to be consulted on policy matters and would not likely tolerate a situation in which it was repeatedly ignored on important issues. The commentary from a board member, who was concerned about board-superintendent relationship, is illuminating:

> I am not sure what my role should be. Business-oriented groups like ours may impose upon the school our own values thereby reducing its capacity to change. That's one that bothers me. We are not taking a hard enough look year by year at what we ought to be doing and I suppose we should ask the superintendent to shock us out of our complacency.

Colleagues on the board were always seen as compatible, and not one adverse comment was recorded by any board member about his fellow associates. By contrast, factional board members can hardly wait to condemn the motives of members from rival factions. It appears that personal animosities are not so likely to arise in a situation where the commonality among co-workers is marked. What we have in Statusville is essentially a friendship clique.

In the preceding commentary we attempted to describe a representative status congruent school board, how it came together, and how it managed its affairs. In this context some generalizations gleaned from studying other status congruent boards deserve stating.

The manner in which the selection machinery functions is a good indicator of what type of board to expect. The caucus or like method tends to restrict board membership within the limits defined by the sponsoring agency; whereas the election process, if uninterfered with, permits a wider range of candidates. The caucus system generally prohibits representatives from special interest groups; and if members are chosen to represent minority groups, they are picked precisely because they do not conform to the minority stereotype. On the other hand, when selection depends on the vote of the mass public, board members may be elected primarily because they are visible and articulate representatives of a particular interest group. Status congruent boards are self-perpetuating bodies in the sense that they are selected by nominating caucuses rather than candidates by choice. The regular election process is purely pro forma.

The interactions which occur within the social system of the status congruent board are warm and friendly. Each member is accorded equal status and is expected to vote his conscience rather than defer to the wishes of a group he supposedly represents. As one particularly vivacious lady board member said:

> The closest we have come to a fight is about girls' clubs. They choose their membership and they are chosen on a ruling clique basis. We are going to see if we can bring this closer to the democratic process. I feel that this is a wrong thing. I am against sororities and fraternities at the college level; at the high school level it is just too darn bad. I would like to force this issue a little faster.

Protocol on the status congruent board is so well established that no board member would embarrass his colleagues by introducing a topic likely to inflame passions, except informally or at private sessions. The social codes of primary groups, as status congruent boards certainly are, do not encourage gauche behavior.

Board meetings themselves are models of parliamentary efficiency. The board president knows his responsibility is to dispense with the agenda as quickly as possible. Difficult topics have been thoroughly aired by community-wide ad-

visory groups and a consensus arrived at before a formal
meeting. Votes are, therefore, generally unanimous though
occasionally a board member may vote against a motion as a
matter of principle. The status congruent board, however,
would not bring a "hot" issue to the floor if many of the
board members were undecided about how to vote. One
should not be misled by the appearance of unanimity in formal sessions; a good deal of extensive debate has occurred in
other settings. The board wishes to assure its public that it
knows what it is doing and that there is no doubt about it.

Status congruent board members usually serve for limited
terms of office; the practice is to remain on the board for two
terms only. Paternalism is thus avoided and more people are
given the opportunity to serve. In any event the caucus system
assures that real deviants never win.

Finally, status congruent boards have the courage of
their convictions. Local school superintendents are much more
subject to threats and backlash tendencies than are state and
federal officials because the former are imprisoned in a social
structure which is eminently visible and can be attacked
readily. The prestigous school board sure of its ground can
withstand these temporary blows with impunity while a less
substantial body might go running for cover at the first sign
of hostilities.

8

THE
TEXTBOOK
SUPERINTENDENT

Whereas the functionary type of superintendent may be classified primarily as a caretaker, as a man who sees his task as keeping the school system functioning smoothly and effortlessly if not creatively, just the opposite behavior is expected of the professional advisor. As an ideal type, the professional advisor is the executive who concentrates on institutional improvement, not by compulsively exerting energy on short-term glamour exploits but rather by concentrating on long-term reordering tasks. The professional advisor is a liberally educated man with humanistic values who at the same time is politically astute, goal oriented, and dedicated to educational statesmanship. Instead of trying to keep the boat from rocking, he is eager for substantive change. Such an ideal leader is probably more legendary than real; nevertheless, the professional literature persistently sets this model up as preferential.

It is our contention that a school community cannot attract or hold men with leadership ability unless it guarantees them reasonable freedom from anxiety about unseemly demands produced by the vicissitudes of community conflict. Where does one find the professional advisor? Unfortunately there is much truth to the aphorism that a community gets what it deserves in the way of a school superintendent. Most of the exquisitely skilled educational practitioners are not found in the big urban complexes or in rural villages where they are badly needed; they are more likely to be discovered in suburban lighthouse districts. There are good explanations for this recurring phenomenon. Probably the most important determinant of local school tax support is the socio-economic character of the community; not fiscal independence, and not the local power structure.[1]

A proven man is able to choose within limits where he wishes to work; he is not obliged to accept what he can get. Therefore, successful superintendents make appraisals of community environments to find out if it is possible to build a school system which will have a reasonable chance of meeting public expectations before they accept a position. Commonsense rubrics apply: good men seek enterprising communities. The most important implication of this practice is that the school community for which the superintendent works is as responsible for his success or failure as the superintendent himself.

Whether one accepts the proposition that leadership is an art, a science, or both, it is certain that administrative experience in some substantial capacity is needed before senior colleagues and board members are likely to respond positively to the leadership attempts of a superintendent of schools. We agree with Barnard that authority is socially derived.[2] Confidence in the rationality, integrity, and intellectual ability of a professional advisor gradually permits him to acquire the support both internally and externally that he needs to move an organization forward. He cannot do it by fiat; hierarchical dominance may work well in certain circumstances but not in collegial educational systems.

Of course, no administrator can rely entirely upon the rationality of his constituency and the impartial review of his employer, the board of education. Management of an educational institution is essentially a political task; therefore, thoroughly safe school systems do not exist in the real world. As we shall see later, even a progressive community occasionally turns down a bond issue.

The professional advisor instinctively senses this fact and he puts a great deal of effort into testing and retesting community reaction to proposals for change. He would never try to surprise a community by taking an action before the majority of public opinion had been prepared and convinced of its propriety.

It is interesting to see how one pluralistic community treats its superintendent. Perfectionville is a predominantly residential community near a large city. It is clearly no ordinary, split-level suburb. Even the most casual visitor would be quick to point out the absence of closely-spaced, look-alike houses and apartments. Other differences, not so obvious, are even more important. Perfectionville has reached a high degree of stability. An unusually large number of residents belong to the managerial and professional class, a fact which has profound and far-reaching effects upon the school system. These people value good education, and impart this sense of value to their children. Highly sophisticated, they are neither stampeded by witch hunts nor impressed by the "newest" educational gimmicks.

A clear-cut statement defining board policies and administrative decision-making areas written years ago is constantly being up-dated. It serves to delineate responsibilities and is carefully adhered to by all groups and individuals.

This is a community which prides itself on its use of extensive citizens' committees whenever any issue of import arises. The citizens are affluent ($40,000 is a minimum home), educated, well-versed in rational decision-making, almost a model of what pluralism represents. There is enough yeast in the community to sharpen issues without splitting people into persistent pros and cons. Leadership comes from a wide variety of sources and everyone who is interested has his say. Cooperation is built into the system.

Board members speak highly of each other, and it appears to be due to a general mutual respect. The board is composed of persons of high social standing. The members are independent and secure. They are able to think and decide as individuals. The board uses community groups to do much staff work and sell its programs to the community.

The superintendent knows his business thoroughly. He has surrounded himself with excellent advisors. When he makes a recommendation, it is well-supported. He carries with him a record of long and competent service. He is a flexible person who relies on knowledge as well as technique and he is always carefully listened to. He expressed his working relationship with the board in these terms:

> It's usually a matter of timing when you work with a board. I made a recommendation to the board before this board came in, the three new members around now. I made a

recommendation to them on a school site last June. Well,
I didn't ask for action. I knew that I wouldn't get action
then with the three members going off. What was on the
record was the fact that I had made the recommendation.
They knew how I stood but they knew I was not pushing
them for a decision. I knew that they needed more information than I had given them, and that's why we arranged these additional meetings and provide additional
information so that they can vote more intelligently.

The superintendent is cognizant of the peculiarities of
each board member and the various eddies and currents in
his community but he uses this information sensitively, ra-
tionally. He is too idealistic and gifted with practical wisdom
to fall into the trap of opportunism. If he did, he would fail
miserably; the fluid nature of the community would make
such a role very dangerous for him. One of his board members views him in the following way:

> He's a good superintendent because he does not give the
> appearance of being an extreme pioneer and yet at the
> same time he gets the pioneering work done. He has kept
> Perfectionville fairly much in the forefront of educational
> developments without upsetting a number of members of
> this community that can be very conservative if they want
> to and many do want to. Pioneering is done one or two
> levels down or through advisory committees and he ap-
> pears to accept their recommendations. Knowing him, the
> initial impetus is put there by him in the first place. His
> success had been due to a very large extent to his fine sense
> of what this community will accept without too much of
> an uproar and he never gives himself the appearance of
> being way out in front but lets the things be done in a
> deliberate way after enough discussion and education of
> the community so that they are at least accepted.

Naturally a superintendent of this caliber makes a lot of important operating decisions but on critical issues of policy he is clearly an advisor. The board is too active to permit him to have his own way without its approval. Of course, since the board's prerogatives and the superintendent's are so clearly delineated in the policy handbook, it would be difficult for the superintendent to overstep his area of jurisdiction.

A female board member aptly summed up the superintendent's administrative style:

> Our superintendent is a master in handling people. He wouldn't precipitate an issue which would split the board. He is very good at timing. What I admire about him the most—you might think he would compromise for expediency. This he has never done. If he feels the issue is right he will go ahead. You never get the feeling that here is an arbitrary man.

It is not true, however, that every economically advantaged suburban school system is successful in locating a prototypic professional advisor. Louis H. Masotti's careful study of New Trier is an example of what happens when a superintendent loses contact with his constituents.[3] New Trier is a high school district encompassing the most affluent northern suburbs of Chicago: Glencoe, Wilmette, Winnetka, and Kenilworth. Its population is composed almost exclusively of upper-status social and economic groups. Its seven board members are elected for three-year terms by popular vote at a non-partisan spring election. The principle of democratic representation is supposedly maintained by a community caucus that recommends candidates to the electorate; these candidates generally run unopposed. All of the school board members represent people of substance in the area; for the

most part long-term residents, Republicans, economically secure, active participants in community life, and prime examples of the dominant social groups. New Trier is like
Perfectionville in almost every respect.

But as Masotti describes a decision-making fiasco at New
Trier, there is no question where the problem lies; it is in
the superintendent's style, not the board members' intransigence. Superintendent Cornog lacked one essential ingredient,
political savvy. The decision to condemn twenty-nine expensive homes in order to establish a few acres of school play-
fields signified a total insensitivity to public opinion.
Moreover, when this decision was put before the voters an attempt was made to jam the issue down the voters' throats in a
highly authoritarian manner. No one questioned Cornog's
intellectual competence; he showed himself to be a brilliant
defender of traditional college preparatory curricula. His mistake was to expect the community to support superior education at any cost and without due explanation. Massoti sums
up the board-superintendent relationship succinctly:

> Cornog's authority in purely educational policy choices is
> unchallenged, and indeed is enhanced by the increasing
> number of these that must be made. Cornog's power in
> the system rests on the Board's reliance upon him to choose
> from among the educationally feasible alternatives in the
> process of declaring major policy goals. That is, he vir-
> tually determines which proposals shall be submitted to
> the voters for approval, and thus controls the agenda of
> community controversy for the education system.[4]

This framework enabled Cornog to advance a proposal for a
second four-year high school even though such a decision was
destined to divide the community. Superintendent Cornog

lacked political skills and he was unable to persuade the community of the desirability of his proposal. Finally, after the leading citizenry became involved in the difficult task of building community support the voters approved the decision to build separate high schools. Cornog was effectively removed from an active role in this essential activity. If the New Trier board of education had not been composed of rational men and women who can accept defeat gracefully, Superintendent Cornog might logically have been forced to resign. Such a gross error in judgment exercised in a less hospitable environment would probably not have been tolerated.

Superintendents holding positions in pluralistic communities over a long period may tend to gravitate toward a decision-making role. Obviously this transition could not be accomplished in a heavy-handed way. New Trier is illustrative of how a skillful superintendent may gain in reputation:

> During the long tenure of Superintendent Gaffney, he was able to combine his educational training and knowledge with community dependence to centralize leadership and authority in the office of the superintendent. Gaffney provided the leadership necessary to make New Trier a system of recognized excellence. His role was recognized by citizens and trustees alike and, as a result, authority within the system came to reside in the superintendent's office.[5]

While some superintendents may "test" the board on the degree to which they can exercise control over its decisions, the role of the professional advisor, once it has come to be accepted both by the board and the superintendent, implies a conscious avoidance of overt policy-making or decision-making on the part of the superintendent. To the extent that the status congruent board will be satisfied with its superintendent, it will see him as avoiding roles they do not expect him to play. This varies somewhat from one community to another, and the perception of it varies from one board member to another. Status congruent board members do not wish to front either for community leaders, for special groups, or for the superintendent. The concern of bright board members in this undeniably tricky area is illuminated by a commentary made by one of them:

> We are not always included in certain matters that I would like to get myself into. That's one that bothers me. I don't know where we should say 'that's the administrator's job' and 'that's one the school board should get into.' The line of demarcation gets difficult in curriculum, student social, athletic, and discipline problems, faculty and administrative organization, and even such items as recruitment of teachers.

For the most part, superintendents who stayed out of policy matters were complimented for doing so by members of status congruent boards. Some members, however, felt ambivalent about this:

> *Interviewer:* How strong a role do you feel that your superintendent plays in the decision-making process on the board?
> *Respondent:* It's a matter of policy. Practically none, to the point where it's almost unhelpful. Even if you ask a direct question, what is your position on this, he will state that it is a matter of policy and the board establishes the policy. The assistant superintendents are a little more helpful. But the superintendent himself tries hard not to influence board procedures that are not in the administrative realm.

Distinctions between the decision-making roles played by superintendents are difficult to determine on the basis of his behavior alone. Much depends upon how the board operates, how it views the superintendent, and what it expects of him, all of which is consistent with the sociological concept of a role as a set of expectations to which a person must conform.

We have observed that members of a status congruent board may fluctuate between allowing their superintendent to be a decision-maker and expecting him to be a professional advisor. When the community viewpoint seems to be fairly well unified, then differences with the superintendent are simply matters of protocol; but, on the other hand, when the community is in considerable disagreement, the recommendations of the superintendent may be questioned more sharply.

The following quotation from a board member defines the preferred role:

> What usually happens is that we listen very carefully to the superintendent and his staff's recommendations and thought, but we make up our own minds. However, when there is a disagreement we tend to accept the superintendent's viewpoints, after all he is an educator and we are not. He is trained in school matters and we are not. We've had disagreements in budgetary matters; the staff has recommended items which I'm sure they thought were important and necessary but which we thought were frills and we have struck them out. We told them to "make do" with what they got particularly this year where we faced a big budget. We try to think for ourselves but at the same time we don't want to make the superintendent or the staff feel that we are "know it all" and we're going to run things our way. We try very much to have as smooth a working organization as we can. There was one situation in which

I was called on the phone by the superintendent's secretary who gave me some order to do something or other and I just said, 'No, I'll make up my mind on this myself.' I think definitely that the superintendent realized right then and there that we're not going to be a rubber stamp board. We're as friendly with them as we can be and go along with every one of their suggestions up to the point where they begin to think that 'They'll sign anything,' and then we take a second look. I think it's worked out very well and our relationship is good—I have the greatest respect for all the members of the superintendent's staff.

One can hardly avoid the view that today's educational administrator is engulfed in a pressure-packed set of constraints. Relative affluence and the growth of strong labor unions have strengthened the hand of the classroom teacher. The clients in the public school system, the students, are beginning to challenge authority in much the same way as their college brethren. Value conflict, or the generational gap if you prefer, is rampant. The role of the professional advisor is becoming much harder to play since it depends on a process as a means to an end. Faced with these winds of change the professional advisor may find himself hopelessly entangled in protracted negotiations, court trials, building programs, having to defend rational persuasion against rebellious tactics, and the like. Instructional improvement may indeed be submerged under these multiple influences.

Many are swept under by the tide of events. An example is President Perkins of Cornell who was victimized when a small band of resisters immobilized his University. President Perkins perceived himself to be a professional advisor but he did not meet his own prescription when faced with a determined force of dissident students.[6] In fact, it is abundantly clear that he did not believe that students should have a real part in the governance of a University. Neither is it surprising that President Stahr of Indiana quit his post with the forthright statement that he saw no reason why he should live his life upside down. The administration of higher education is becoming similar to public school administration.

There are public school administrators who have demonstrated the ability to overcome severe obstacles without becoming debilitated or defeated. It is not an easy assignment and good mental health is an absolute prerequisite. In truth, professional advisors are few and far between these days.

We have been challenged by the dilemma often simplistically stated as the leadership dilemma. Is it circumstances which determine success or is it administrative acumen? Answers to this question are exceedingly complex.

We know, for instance, that state aid for schools is nearly one hundred percent additive to local tax effort in suburban districts, while it is less than this—perhaps around 70 percent additive—in large central city districts.[7] Since the amount of per pupil aid received on the average by suburban school districts is greater than that received by large city districts, and since aid is one hundred percent additive in suburban districts, increases in state aid without formula modifications will increase rather than close the gap in educational expenditures between city and suburb.

There is little question that wealthy suburban districts, more properly called privileged cultural islands, are advantaged under current state laws and regulations. These elite and mature suburban communities, and by this definition we exclude upward-mobile-striving habitats such as Park Forest, Illinois, are relatively homogeneous in life style and generally tend toward a high consensus mentality. As one board member in such a community stated:

> We assume that the majority of people moving here do so because of the schools and, being in the economic category which they have to be in, we assume that they want the finest in education and physical facilities. We don't carry that assumption so far as to be reckless. We are pretty sure that the greatest majority are interested in the finest things in life. Education is one. That is why our school has the reputation that it has.

Our sample included a number of first-rate suburban school systems. The administrators of these advantaged institutions were men of uncommon abilities. This is not to say that their behavior was identical; some veered toward adjustment, others toward idiosyncratic and often rebellious behavior, but the most successful, if one means by this statement universal acclaim, relied heavily on what is euphemistically referred to as public relations. Canadian suburbs seem to have captured the American attitude to some degree; note what a Crestwood Heights teacher has to say about her superintendent:

> A sort of esprit de corps has been fostered here in a democratic way, for example, when forming policy, etc. We haven't a dictator for a head. All opinions are respected and we are encouraged to contribute ideas. This feeling of an esprit de corps brings out the best in you. You don't feel as if you are just a cog in a machine, but an important member of a going concern. A teacher feels that if he falls down he is letting the school down. . . . The har-

mony is real, it is not just a front and I think I have been
here long enough to say that. It can be mainly attributed
to the principal and the director of education; the director really has the knack of working with people.[8]

Much is expected of the modern-day school superintendent. While fiction prescribes that he is heading up a non-
political community-oriented institution similar to a religious
institution, reality offers a less inspiring picture. When we
remove our ideological glasses, we are confronted with a
highly politicized situation. School systems are not sanctu-
aries like monasteries; they are the warp and woof of local
politics.

Neither intellectual arrogance nor casuistry are assets to
the highly professional advisor. Status congruent communities
prefer a superintendent who has learned the lessons of cooperative decision-making, the *sine qua non* of modern-day
business practice. Winston Churchill had charisma of an unusual order, inspired and sustained by the nation's desperate
need for survival; few school communities are looking for
this order of directive leadership. Pluralistic environments
will ultimately be enraged by unilateral decisions, irrespective
of the intrinsic merit involved. The professional advisor facing a school crisis is wise to rely upon broad-based community-wide support.

The single formula as a magic key permeates the educational enterprise. We are constantly seeking the approach
which will somehow solve our educational problems; all too
often these fads run in cycles and repeat themselves over
time. Today's panacea may become tomorrow's discard. Administering such illogical and confused organizations is indeed

a hazardous occupation. The true professional advisor is subjected to enormous pressures to conform to the role of maintenance specialist. Public opinion is not geared to rapid educational innovation; it is frightened and upset by the very thought of a new dimension in this hallowed specialty. Weak men succumb to the pressures; politically astute individuals play the game; leaders fight the system. Obviously a professional advisor can only succeed where citizens are secure enough to tolerate inventive ideas; these places are unfortunately rare.

Research on leadership tells us that the administrator has more freedom to establish his own job responsibilities the higher up the hierarchy he moves; the greater the uncertainty in the tasks he faces, the greater the discretion he has.[9]

Few would dispute that the school superintendent's environment is uncertain; it is also apparent that he holds the most visible hierarchical position in the school system. If a crisis develops, he will be immediately the center of the controversy. In short, he occupies a highly vulnerable role.

The superintendent who is a professional advisor is in the best position to survive the rude shocks of ill fortune. He is supported by a board of education composed of solid citizens who will not quake at the first sign of discontent. James Coleman in his well-known essay on community conflict pointed out how powerful support by outstanding members of the Scarsdale community prevented a "burning of the books" debacle.[10]

Since the professional advisor reads widely in his field, he is able to increase his discretionary influence by the sheer weight of his special knowledge. But this does not mean he can act as an autocrat; he is required to demonstrate that his choices are reasonable and he must build support with his board and with leading citizens in the community. In an uncertain environment, it takes unusual talent and ingenuity to play this role successfully. Fortunately for society, there are men who are able to live up to these high expectations.

NOTES

1. Seymour Sacks, "Central City and Suburban Public Education: Fiscal Resources and Fiscal Realities," in Robert J. Havighurst, ed., *1968 NSSE Yearbook: Educational Metropolitanism,* Chicago: National Society for the Study of Education, 1968.

2. Chester I. Barnard, *The Functions of the Executive,* Cambridge, Massachusetts: Harvard University Press, 1945.

3. Louis Masotti, *Education and Politics in Suburbia: The New Trier Experience,* Cleveland: The Press of Western Reserve University, 1967.

4. Ibid., pp. 155–56.

5. Ibid., p. 155.

6. James A. Perkins, *The University in Transition,* Princeton: Princeton University Press, 1966, p. 90.

7. Alan K. Campbell, "Educational Policy-Making Studied in Large Cities," *American School Board Journal,* March, 1967, pp. 16–24.

8. John R. Seeley, R. Alexander Sim, and Elizabeth W. Loosely, *Crestwood Heights: A Study of the Culture of Suburban Life,* New York: John Wiley and Sons, 1956, p. 505.

9. Dennis Palumbo, "Power and Role Specificity in Or-

ganization Theory," *Public Administration Review,* 29, May–June, 1969, pp. 237–48.

10. James S. Coleman, *Community Conflict,* Glencoe, Illinois: The Free Press, 1957, p. 32.

PART FIVE

THE INERT COMMUNITY, THE SANCTIONING BOARD, AND THE SUPERINTENDENT AS DECISION-MAKER

In many communities the flow of power on issues regarding the school system is reversed from that found in the three types discussed in the previous three sections. Here, the super-intendent is a decision-maker—he quietly sets policy and sees to it that it is implemented. He is viewed as the expert.

This occurs when the board of education simply sanctions what the superintendent suggests, abnegating its formal responsibility for policy.

And how can a board function simply as a sanctioning instrument for the superintendent? It appears that such conditions exist in communities lacking any apparent power structure, at least as far as school issues are concerned.

9

APATHY
AND THE
RUBBER STAMP

In many communities we find no discernibly structured power or influence flowing from the community to community-wide boards, and no apparent control of professionals emanating from either the community or a board. Among the fifty-one communities in our study, thirteen were classified as inert; the inert community, in fact, was the second most frequent type encountered. No claim is made that this distribution indicates the frequency with which inert types might be expected to be found in a national sample of American communities. Our research sought answers to a different set of questions. Still it is reasonable to assume that there are a large number of inert communities in our society, particularly in rural areas. Unfortunately, the agonies torturing our system of public education today are utterly beyond the capacity of these places to resolve them even if they so wished.

In our thirteen inert communities, we found eight boards of education that acted simply as rubber stamp sanctions for the superintendent, with no apparent influence stemming directly from the community. In the other five situations, one board was controlled by an individual who initiated most of the decisive actions within the board, although he had no power base in the community at large. Another board was factional, but again with no supporting community factions; the split was apparently caused by personal animosities. The other three boards were composed of active and interested citizens who interacted in much the same fashion as our status congruent boards.

The existence of various types of boards in the inert community is understandable since there is no community pressure to impose any form of relationship within a board.

Indeed, our model suggests that a sanctioning board will likely emerge in an inert community; this, while generally true we also found countered in a number of cases. This fact in itself supports the thesis that the power structure of the community or its absence determines to a considerable extent the interrelationships among board members. The expectations placed upon boards in dominated, factional, and pluralistic structures are clearly understood by all parties concerned. But in the inert structure explicit expectation is lacking.

It is important to note that the inert classification does not presume the complete absence of power relations. Within every institutional order, we find power relations existing. Employers still manage their employees; parents still supervise their children; nurses are subordinate to physicians; and political office usually carries with it influences that are not officially delegated to that position. Moreover, political roles such as the mayor or city manager may carry with them patterns of power similar to those ascribed to religious spokesmen.

In this atmosphere, the professional plays the role of the decision maker.

The responses to interviews from the inert community and the sanctioning board differ considerably from those in the other communities; their answers are very short. While respondents do answer questions directly, they offer few clues as to the existence of power and conflict in the community. In many interviews with sanctioning board members and inert community power figures (potential power figures) the interviewer did almost as much talking as the respondent.

This style is indicated in the following interview which illustrates how one superintendent performs the role of decision-maker:

> *Respondent:* I think the main thing on whether board members talk very much or not is because of the superintendent. The superintendent makes so much difference.
> *Interviewer:* He does?
> *Respondent:* Yes, in a board meeting.
> *Interviewer:* Does the superintendent take an active lead in the meetings?
> *Respondent:* Usually.
> *Interviewer:* Does he make a lot of recommendations and that sort of thing?
> *Respondent:* Oh, yes.
> *Interviewer:* Do you usually accept them?
> *Respondent:* Oh, I wouldn't say all of them but quite a few of them. This fellow we have right now, why I think he's real good as a superintendent. He weighs everything real carefully before he suggests any changes.

What contributes to a "powerless" power structure? The very statement seems to be a contradiction in terms. Does it actually exist or are we deluding ourselves? First, we must examine the possibility that our methods were not sensitive enough to discover a possible underlying reality. The reader will remember that communities were classified as inert only after a uniform set of interviews found no evidence of power relations, conflict, or organized activities in connection with school activities. It is hard to dispute hard data of this kind, particularly when it has been scrupulously collected by competent interviewers.

One factor leading to inertness is ideological homogeneity. Citizens see themselves as equals with similar interests, values, and goals. One such community led one of our interviewers to remark: "Ashville is so dominated it is inert." Given these conditions the inert structure is highly probable, provided of course no one person or group is attributed the status of "watchdog."

A second contributing factor is resignation. Many small rural communities are characterized by a seeming purposelessness; improvement of their living conditions is simply beyond their imagining.

A third factor is that organized activity may be confined to one institution only, resulting in inertness elsewhere. For example, we discovered a community which spent all its energy in seeking new industries to the neglect of other interests including schools.

In almost any community certain persons or groups can be found with a potential for power. Here we are concerned with the actual operation of power, and we have chosen the term inert to describe a situation where specific power relations did not develop into precise patterns. The term inert remains appropriate if one attaches to it the concept of potential power, power present but dormant. In other words, we hold that the complete absence of power is an untenable notion. The inert structure is not a zero point; it is an amorphous structure. The inert community is probably best understood in terms of the frontier philosophy enshrined in our value structure—that individuals are responsible for their own welfare, and that organizational success is the result of individual leadership.

Both the notion of social structure as an entity and organized activity as essential to community progress are absent in the individualistic philosophy of the inert community. The parent-teachers organization is viewed as an aggregate of individual parents; the community is viewed in terms of relatively apathetic individuals, and the channels through which a satisfactory educational system can be achieved are for the most part personal—the complaints and criticism of individuals.

Each community in our sample was classified by our field interviewers in terms of the specified models. These evaluations included the rejection of types as well as the sureness of "fit" between the community and the model. It is especially important in the case of the inert community to show how this was done. (The rejection of the other types of community structure is tantamount to admitting inertness.) Following is the field report filed on a small community, one in which there had been a consolidation of two school districts. Often such a centralization results in factionalism, but in this instance it did not.

I. The Community Classified

A.   The interviewing team rejects the dominant classification because:

    1. There is no main industry except farming, although there are a few strong farm-service type business-men.

    2. No single strong figure or group was identified through the interviews. No group or individual seems to consistently influence any local policy.

    3. No strong formal organizations are present in the community.

    4. Interviews with board members indicate that there is no consistent or strong external influence or interest in board activity.

B. The team rejects the factional classification because:

    1. No rural-town split was evident, and no other "objective" basis for power.

    2. There is no apparent antagonism between the two towns regarding educational policies. Most respondents regard the relationship as one of cooperation, but it appears mainly to be the absence of interest.

C. The team rejects the pluralistic classification because:

    1. The respondents indicate that, in general, the community respects the superintendent and values his recommendations highly.

    2. The community is generally Republican and/or conservative, although politics do not enter into school board elections. Campaigns are never hotly contested.

D. Therefore, the team accepts the inert classification because:

    1. The respondents indicate that it is difficult to get people to run for the school board.

2. Only one board recommendation since consolidation, a bond issue, has been rejected by the community. The respondents blame the defeat at the polls on general apathy regarding building needs and a reluctance to accept a tax rate increase, plus a rainy election day. Although one possible power figure, a businessman, Mr. Owens, was identified, he was not actively concerned with educational policy or board activities, so far as we could determine. He was actively opposed to the bond issue and may have influenced the vote. This was, however, a matter of taxes rather than educational policy.

3. No apparent active community interest in educational policies was evident nor was there any active interest in the board's or superintendent's activities.

II. Board Classification

A. The team rejects the dominated board classification because:

1. No connections nor consultations between the board members and local power figures were indicated, nor is there any particularly strong or influential board member.

2. There is no evidence of board members being endorsed or nominated by any individual, group, or power figures.

B. The team rejects the factional board classification because:

1. Although membership is made up of three each from

the two towns, there was no evidence of voting on issues along town lines.

2. Votes were almost always unanimous and discussion almost never occurs.

3. The board is characterized by long-range stability and cooperation and changes in membership seldom affect board operation.

4. There seem to be no preconceived viewpoints prior to actually voting on issues. Discussion concerning issues is the rule rather than the exception.

C. The team rejects the status-congruent classification because:

1. Although the board members seem to regard each other as colleagues, the superintendent's recommendations and policies have seldom been rejected. The board looks to him for leadership.

2. Board membership changes through voluntary resignation rather than through defeat at the polls.

3. Issues are resolved through unanimous vote.

4. There is a general reluctance to accept candidacy in the community for membership on the board. Members do not seem to represent any particular viewpoints or community interests.

5. "What's best for the school system" is defined by the superintendent.

D. Therefore, the team accepts the sanctioning board classification because:

1. The respondents consistently indicate that the board looks to the superintendent for leadership and accepts his recommendations.

2. There is no strong leadership on the board, including the chairman.
3. The superintendent indicated that the board has accepted 99 percent of his proposals over the past five years.
4. The board does not consult with community leaders but rather tends to turn to the superintendent for guidance, information, and leadership.

III. Superintendent Classification

A. The team rejects the functionary classification because:
1. His recommendations are accepted 99 percent of the time by the board, according to his statement, which seems to be supported by board statements.
2. He does not consult with community leaders to any great extent.

B. The team rejects the political manipulator classification because:
1. There are no apparent factions to manipulate and he does not consult with board members informally.

C. The team rejects the professional advisor classification because:
1. His statement that there are only a few special meetings and in many cases there is no point in calling these people in on every little detail.
2. The board seems to value his professional knowledge highly and seldom deviates from his proposals.

D. Therefore, the team accepts the decision-maker classification because:

1. He indicates that most proposals are carefully laid out by himself and his staff prior to their presentation to the board.
2. Once again, 99 percent of his proposals were accepted by the board.
3. At least one board member indicated dissatisfaction with a particular policy (introduction of the "new" math method) but he nevertheless voted for it.
4. The superintendent states, "No problems with my board," and that he has a "Utopian situation" and "I'm very fortunate."
5. He does not consistently consult with the community leaders.

We have selected as our example a city of about 25,000 in which certain persons had expended great effort to obtain power in the community, an endeavor which had met with little success. For many years, this city had been inactive and unconcerned; it could be characterized as dull and defeated. The superintendent had been in office for twenty-nine years and was ready to retire. Such long tenure is typical of the decision-maker in a truly inert community. An elementary school was named after him, which is also par for the course in such cases.

The living standard was average or slightly below average on a national scale. There was a minority group in the community, but this group, although physically visible, was geographically isolated in a small area with a different name, and received little attention from the people in the core community.

The superintendent of schools made certain that no issue

came up that would raise the ire of any board member or any local segment of the community. Therefore, there was very little in the way of controversy, argument, debate, or the like, on the sanctioning school board. School board meetings were very short since they were confined to approving the recommendations of the superintendent.

This superintendent did not play a hard-fisted, desk-pounding authoritarian role. Rather, much of his work was done behind the scenes. He frequently contacted board members on issues and probably knew exactly how every vote would go beforehand. This allowed him the option of failing to bring up issues that might lead to a confrontation or raise some question regarding his authority.

The school board members felt that Dr. X knew school matters well. He had a doctor's degree and long experience with the schools. Why should they question him? Or, as it was more often put, "Who am I to question him?" It was also felt that he did a good job, and by comparison with surrounding schools this opinion was unquestionably true. There had been slow but sure progress in implementing modern educational policy. Improvements were made, but conspicuous issues such as sex education, additional vocational courses, and bond issues on new schools were brought up only after the superintendent was relatively assured that everyone agreed on them. The principals in the elementary and junior high schools "ran their schools." There was almost no difficulty between teachers and parents that could not be handled by each principal. The counselors, administrative assistants, principals, or any person involved in any way in school policy were all hand-picked by the superintendent.

Perhaps the key issue in the decision-maker role is that of selecting board members. In this community two methods were used. The school board itself urged people to run for the school board, and they usually did so unopposed. School board members reported that candidates were always suggested by the superintendent. The suggestion was made in terms of the name, the person's prestige in the community, his talent for being down-to-earth on crucial issues, and his compatibility with the other board members. Furthermore, when citizen committees were necessary, the appointment was made by the board—again, always at the suggestion of the superintendent as to who would be interested, competent, and willing to serve. Even when opposing candidates ran, there was always an urgency on the part of citizens just before the election to determine how the superintendent felt about each candidate. He never openly took sides, but it was well known throughout the community whom he supported. Sex education was provided in the school finally, but not until just before a study took place in which letters were sent home with each child for parents to sign. The way had been cleared because it was strongly recommended by all of the parent-teacher associations in town. Sex education caused the superintendent some consternation, as he reported to us; but since the parents wanted it, he felt that he could always refer the more vocal opposition to the various presidents of the local parent-teacher associations.

One threat which the inert community faces is the increasing probability of more militance among teachers. The following interview indicates how a sanctioning board member views the matter:

Interviewer: How are your teachers organized?

Respondent: Well, I would say that 98 percent of them either belong to the American Federation of Teachers or the State Education Association and both organizations are working very hard toward higher salaries and better working conditions. One of our chief problems is the AFT. It is following union tactics and really not using any basic reasoning in its demands for increased salaries and more favorable working conditions. During the last salary meeting, the AFT brought up about three points concerning salary and in each case these three points had been acted on last year and the increase had been granted. This year during salary discussion the AFT asked for double what they received last year. In other words, no rhyme or reason, but just double, and we as board members simply can't double anyone's salary. They are using union tactics. That's what I say. If they want a fifty cent raise, they ask for a dollar raise and hope that they will end up somewhere in between. Up until recently we have not had to contend with that type of deal. But that will be standard procedure in the near future.

Interviewer: Does the AFT carry much weight in the community?

Respondent: No, not necessarily in the community but they are beginning to make a showing on the teacher personnel. They are beginning to make their presence felt.

There was a time in the not too distant past when the management of schools was routine enough to permit part-time lay amateurs to gain satisfaction from the position. The sanctioning board had some of the conviviality of a country club. One respondent wistfully told this story:

I like to go to board meetings; it is a chance to shave, get dressed up, and shoot the breeze with your friends. One of us brings a pie or two and the superintendent has coffee ready. Very rarely do we have visitors at the meetings, so we sit around and relax. The superintendent takes his time getting through the agenda. If I were off the board, I would really miss it.

Boards that are willing to permit their superintendents to exercise almost full responsibility for operating the school system are usually composed of men who are not accustomed to the accountability techniques employed by industry. Ordinarily, there is trust of monumental proportions. One veteran board member had tears in his eyes when he gave this testimonial:

Prof has been here for as many years as I can remember. He knows every kid in school by his first name and he never misses a church supper. Every minister in town sings his praises. He even coaches little league baseball in summer free of charge. I would never question his recommendation if I knew he had his heart set on it. Of course, sometimes he is not sure of his ground and he asks us for our opinion. He realizes that we get around the community a little easier than he does; we keep both ears to the ground and if we hear any rumblings we let him know immediately. In no time, the whole issue is resolved. He is an absolute master.

Sanctioning board members are not very interesting to interview. What excitement is there in a recital of pedestrian routine? The issues discussed by such boards are never earthshaking. When asked what controversial issues come up for discussion in a board meeting, a sanctioning member said:

That's a real hard question to answer. Last year there was some dissatisfaction with the basketball coach. He liked to run up the score and some people thought he ought to substitute more. We have had a teacher or two who liked to drink too much. Some want to fire such a person and others believe he is the greatest. Fortunately the boy got dead drunk and was picked up by the local police. Usually the superintendent knows how to handle these matters; he just keeps us informed.

Sanctioning boards do not meet often and their meetings do not last long; there are few items on the agenda. Members prize the informality and dispatch with which they complete their work. A decision-making superintendent had this to say:

> The men on my board work hard all day. None of them know very much about the intricacies of education; few read more than the local newspaper. They are all decent individuals and I never use any pedagese on them. We start at 8:00 P.M. and the meeting is over by 10:00 P.M. They like to look at the bills but they seldom question my judgment. On curriculum matters the idea would never occur to them.

Up to now we have been describing sanctioning boards settled in inert communities. On occasion, factional boards in prominent urban areas defer to a powerful superintendent. For years, Benjamin Willis ran the Chicago public schools as he saw fit with the tacit consent of his board. His last few years, however, were stormy ones; he clearly was out-of-step with the community power structure, but his unsurpassed political acumen enabled him to hold his pivot where lesser men would have been swept out of office.

Our evidence leads us to believe that a sanctioning board may very well be a relic of the past. High taxes, teacher unions, black power, and student insurrections seem to have catapulted even sleepy little towns into the mainstream of American society. Or have they?

10

CHARISMA
AND POWER
BY DEFAULT

Charisma, like serendipity, has become a household word during the past few years. The Weberian idea that some men are endowed with exceptional powers or qualities by which they are able to acquire unusual organizational control, substantiates the speculation that decision-makers exist even in our highly bureaucratized society. Are there also charismatic school superintendents or is this dramatic form of leadership restricted to religious and political figures who rise to fill a special need in times of chaos?

The man who depends upon his invincibility or special "gift of grace" may be drummed out of his leadership role with alacrity once his magic disappears. It is not surprising that most superintendents do not wish to be known publicly as the "boss." It is much safer, and, it may be appropriately said, wiser, to play down one's power base. After all, the superintendent is supposed to be essentially a public official appointed by a board; he does not have a direct political

mandate from the people. In reality, however, the superintendent who wishes to increase his autonomy has to place his
board of education in a sanctioning role as a buffer against
the pressures exerted from outside the organization. Again
and again in our daily experience we have seen public control
act as a great constraint upon radical innovation. Unless the
superintendent can present a persuasive case to the authorities of the public sector, he is not going to get the necessary
resources for implementing change.

Besides toughness and sophistication which are absolute
musts, the ability to become a decision-maker implies that
one man is able to determine a course of action on a critical
issue by virtue of the immense persuasiveness of his argumentation, possibly benefitting from the confidence accruing from
successful past choices, through the sheer disinterest of his
constituency, or by carefully controlling access to the data
sources readily available to an official with a fixed responsibility. Other possibilities exist for the truly Machiavellian
decision-maker of which, we are confident, there are at least
a few around.

Every administrator, if you wish to press the point, is to
a greater or lesser degree a decision-maker. There are always
problems requiring administrative answers and many of these
are never monitored or second-guessed by the board of education or power figures in the community. Even the most
obsequious administrator is granted limited leverage on in-
significant matters. But these stereotypic, bureaucratically oriented choices are no substitute for real power.

While school systems do have superintendents who perform as decision-makers, they are becoming more difficult to
find under the mounting pressure of heavy population mobil-

ity, school reorganization schemes, and the consequent increasing pluralism of American society. It has been customary in rural villages to refer to the superintendent of schools as "prof," a friendly appellation setting the head administrator apart as an acknowledged specialist. If a man chose to spend his lifetime in one of these rural villages, he might very well gain the sincere respect and good will of most of the citizenry; their confidence would permit a man of ability to take virtual command of the schools. His long tenure would contribute to his indispensability; few would dare challenge him in his own bailiwick. In earlier days societal norms were seldom under challenge; discontent centered more on means to ends and the ubiquitous personality clashes that invade any organizational domain.

Few would deny that the forces impinging on today's administrator are intense. The problem of race and the disenchantment of youth have challenged the very survival of educational organizations. This polarization threatens to create a conservative backlash which may cause school systems to be supervised in terms of repressive value frameworks.

In these days of travail, the decision-making superintendent has his hands full. Still, if the community is inactive and unstructured, his expert knowledge enables him to set a reasonably autonomous course; active supervision by his sanctioning board is unlikely. In fact, protected by the mystery of all-powerful state statutes and laws, the superintendent with an urge to run things in accordance with his own concept of education is able, by controlling the agenda of local board meetings, to develop a form of sovereignty over his dominions worthy of an absolute monarch.

On most issues involving the internal dynamics of the

school system, the superintendent has specialized knowledge vastly superior to anyone on the board of education. Such a strategic position allows the decision-making superintendent to give, withhold, or slant information according to his wishes. It gives him a freer hand. As one board member put it:

> Well, the superintendent is our chief source of information because he has been our superintendent now for a long time; he knows the district and he also knows his way around the state educational headquarters in the capitol and he knows his way around the legislative halls as well. He is a rather well-informed individual on any and all educational problems.

Another device used by the decision-maker is to prevent the board from assuming a hard line on issues that might arouse community controversy. One of the best examples that came to our attention relates to dress codes, a subject that in the past decade has become a nationwide issue avidly followed in the press. A member of one of our sanctioning boards had this to say:

> Well, attire is a very touchy question and we have not had to act on it as a board. The principals and our superintendent naturally have bumped into this time and time again, and they have had many meetings on it and they have always resolved it so far. By doing that, the board has not had to expose its hand and say you can or can't wear this or that.

To the extent that the superintendent is intuitively effective in the expert's role, his security is protected. One interesting observation, found almost exclusively in inert communities, was the lack of response in otherwise smooth-running interviews to the question of possibly firing the superintendent. In several interviews in which respondents were open and receptive, answers to this threatening question were unemotional and bland. A blank response could be accounted for by the sheer novelty of the thought, but we interpret these findings to represent a practical legitimation of the decision-maker in his role.

Likewise, the superintendent's name is quickly introduced in inert community interviews and occurs with a frequency not usually found elsewhere. Such an example is found in the following quote:

> *Interviewer:* Do you seek the advice of any friends or community leaders on issues sometimes?
>
> *Respondent:* Well, I've served on the board since the beginning of World War II. Very frequently I have just sat down and tried to devote a half an hour to recalling things when we have faced similar questions in the past, and how they have been resolved. I rely quite heavily on that. The second source of information, as I have said, we have an exceptionally well-balanced, and exceptionally capable superintendent. Very frequently I might have discussion with him pertaining to issues. Seldom do I go to my neighbors; even more seldom do I go to any group of people. I have never—practically never—discussed school issues with a group of people except when it was a uniform plan for the entire district.

The practice of initiating ideas upon request gives the superintendent a tremendous amount of power and leaves him free from any suggestion that he is trying to control the board. The effective decision-maker can utilize such informal contacts, initiated by individual board members, to the fullest extent.

The respect accorded sanctioning board members by other

board members is similar to that found in the status congruent board: differences are discussed quietly and great efforts are made not to offend anyone in the discussion. While mutual respect is also found in the pluralistic community, individuals are sufficiently secure to allow considerable confrontation of ideas as part of the accepted pattern of relations at board meetings. In the inert community, whether suburban or small town, such confrontation would give rise to suspicions of personal mistrust and lack of respect.

An unusually astute awareness of the sanctioning role was evident in some members of pluralistic suburbs: well-educated managers of their own businesses or professionals who supervised other people, were quick to ascertain the intent of questions directed toward determining whether the board was sanctioning.

As one interviewer reported:

After the interview the respondent seemed to be a little more frank, although he had no startling revelations. He did indicate that the superintendent had been in the district for over a decade, was very sharp and as the board member put it, 'a free wheeling individual.' There was every indication that this board member felt that the board tended to follow the superintendent's recommendations, that is, the policy was formulated by the superintendent and simply approved by the board. He mentioned also that the superintendent does not bow to anyone in the community; he knows what is right and carries it out. As an example, the editor of the local newspaper is a member of the American Civil Liberties Union and prior to the baccalaureate service this year wrote a rather scathing editorial insisting that this service was unconstitutional and should be dropped. The superintendent has a weekly article or newsletter in the paper. Immediately following the editorial, the superintendent wrote an equally scathing reply indicating that the service is entirely voluntary, that it did not use public funds and the like. He said they were going to keep it. The service had something like 97 percent attendance. The editor wrote a follow-up article but nothing much happened after that. The superintendent did not refer the letter to the board but acted.on his own in this particular issue.

Through informal discussions at the board meeting a decision-making superintendent may give the impression of open communication. Since he is "on top of everything" the board members have a feeling of freedom within the structure. Note the following comment:

> *Interviewer:* How about communications between the superintendent and the board?
> *Respondent:* Pretty good, pretty good. Matter of fact, we never have a regular meeting that our superintendent doesn't devote at least half an hour to just plain shop-talk —not on any particular item, no agenda or anything— just free discussions from any board member, any question we want to ask the superintendent he will answer.

A significant feature of this process is that it is carried on in response to board member questions, and since board members cannot be completely informed of what is actually going on, the superintendent is in an advantageous position to make decisions. His greater knowledge of facts, expressed values, and potential opposition to any program may, in a sense, overwhelm the board. We are quite certain that this may be unconscious on the part of some superintendents, but our impression is that it may be all the more effective when natural and intuitive rather than contrived through deliberate manipulation.

A suburban school district some thirty minutes by train from a large metropolis sets the stage for our story. Old landed estates (some now divided into large lots), mansioned and secluded, are well represented in the district.

The population is quite homogeneous: Republican (divided into liberal and conservative), wealthy (both old and new wealth), gentile (although twenty percent Jewish), white (two percent black), residential (no industry). It is best described as very wealthy, dotted with numerous private and parochial schools, and with a leg firmly implanted on traditional continental United States.

During the last four years, although the budget has gone up regularly, school taxes have not risen. The increased revenue comes, apparently, from a large office complex being erected in the community plus additional luxury apartments. Zoning is strictly enforced and in most respects has helped to maintain the traditional atmosphere of the area. One third of the eligible children attend private (usually day) schools.

The superintendent has held long tenure in the district and is firmly in the driver's seat. He controls board member selections to a large extent, although not overtly. Note the following responses by the superintendent:

> *Interviewer:* How are board members selected?
> *Superintendent:* We have not had a person elected to this board in 15 to 18 years who got on it from scratch. Somebody resigns and the board appoints a person. Then when his term expires, he runs. Occasionally there are people that run in the primary, but they don't win.
> *Interviewer:* Do you have a real role to play in the selection of new board members?
> *Superintendent:* I have a powerful role but not an identified one. I'm very close to my board members and I

feel very free to talk with them and they consult me individually and collectively. We have a real easy relationship. I don't have a board member that I have a problem with.

Interviewer: How do you directly influence board member selection?

Superintendent: If they were getting real hot on somebody that I knew they better know something about, I'd say, 'Look, you better know this about this person. You still decide but you check this aspect about it.'

The superintendent's power is so great that if it came to any difference between him and the board, he would win. He has even bucked the community and the board on some crucial issues and made his choices stick. He does not have a policy manual, but operates out of his back pocket according to what he considers the best interest of the community. He makes major curriculum and personnel decisions without always consulting the board. The line between formal and informal policy is a thin one, as he likes to run the show. Only the final product is answerable to the board, and very few of the processes along the way are brought to its attention for consideration.

The superintendent is quite open; for instance:

Interviewer: What do you do on tricky personnel problems?

Superintendent: Usually it's just left to me and I sometimes don't even tell the board how it turned out. I've got one going on right now. The board in general knows what the problem is but they don't want to participate in the solution. This is my job. The administrator decides and I've decided. But that doesn't come up at public board meetings. Sometimes I tell the board and sometimes I say nothing. If they incidentally ask me, otherwise I leave it alone.

Interviewer: How would you characterize your activity during the board meeting?

Superintendent: We have a very fixed agenda. We spend a minimum of time on things like bills and that stuff. There's a section of the superintendent's report on everything for discussion. I write out the first portion—its informational, no action. Just to make a record that something happened or to introduce somebody or something of that sort. The second section is items for board action and I basically use three levels of action. One to suggest action on the item. A lot of these items have been processed before. They're not caught unawares—oh, small things like a school calendar—I'll write that out and submit it and if they want to change it, we change it. But if I say suggest that means that I recognize there might be alternative positions quite readily. If I recommend, they know that this is a strong position on the basis of the necessity of a good deal of technical attention and staff work. Under the law I'm free to discuss but not to vote. I do very little talking at a board meeting. The material that I have to say is written. It is written briefly and carefully edited and they know what I mean. Then if they want to ask questions occasionally the president of the board will say, "Well, do you want to amplify this or is one of your staff members prepared to amplify this?"

Interviewer: Then if there are no questions, you go ahead?

Superintendent: We don't have long harangues. The board has good discipline. We're very formal in our addressing one another at board meetings. It's a highly disciplined kind of meeting. Anybody would be reprimanded either there or off the record for a cat-and-dog type engagement.

The superintendent is an intelligent and unusually perceptive man. He works closely with the board members, never alienating himself from them. He takes positions when asked and usually has laid enough groundwork that his recommendations are accepted. He is identified with all board members through social affairs. He is never surprised at what the board members decide.

Listen to a board member's perception:

> *Interviewer:* Is it the superintendent or the president of the board who makes the decisions?
>
> *Board Member:* I would say the superintendent would make the decision that he felt correct but I would also say that if the president of the school board didn't feel that it was correct, he'd be just as quick to say so.
>
> *Interviewer:* And who do you think would prevail?
>
> *Board Member:* The superintendent.
>
> *Interviewer:* How would the superintendent go about resolving the conflict?
>
> *Board Member:* He would call individuals, either the board members themselves, or have someone else do it for him.
>
> *Interviewer:* He has that kind of network?
>
> *Board Member:* You bet. He knows almost to the man or lady on the school board who is going to vote which way and who he has to work on that isn't going the right way at the moment.

Board members were quite aware of the superintendent's almost total control of the decision-making process. As one member put it:

> *Interviewer:* Does the superintendent delegate enough authority?
>
> *Board Member:* He delegates authority but it's never

really delegated because you are always quite sure who is making the final decision. Nobody down to the last man would move without him.

Interviewer: Would this include board members as well?

Board Member: If the board members felt they had to get across a point of view in opposition to him, they would have to move delicately. They would do it very discreetly and very quietly. His protection against this is that he's very well informed and he has his roots down, so as soon as there is a straw in the wind, he's aware and he can begin to adjust. He makes a good intelligent judgment, whether it's important or not and then he gets his staff to do something about it, so that basically it works pretty well.

Perhaps the newspaper editor in town summed up the board-superintendent relationships accurately when he said:

Interviewer: Who has the real levers of power? Superintendent or board members?

Editor: The superintendent.

Interviewer: How does he manage it?

Editor: The superintendent plants the seeds and waters them and grows them and the board, by and large, just smiles and suns on them. I think this is a good design. The board members are competent people in their fields; they do not regard themselves as educators. If they felt the superintendent was incompetent, I think they would do something about it.

The interviewing team working in this community ended its field report with the following observation:

Calling the community inert does not put it in the same category as some of the rural communities previously studied. But it does separate it from communities actively

seeking to better themselves. People are quite satisfied
with the status quo in school affairs. Thus either a dormant pluralism or an organized inertness best describes
the situation. Although the superintendent 'manipulates'
his board, it is not the kind of political manipulation
described in the model. He really acts more as a decision-
maker. The board is a mixture of dominated, sanctioning, and status congruent. Dominated should be rejected
because traditionally this community has defined its board
as a big city board that does not bother itself with most
school operations. In a very limited sense, it is a status
congruent board, debating issues within certain limits,
smaller limits than one would find on most status congruent boards. Incidentally and because of previous ma-
nipulations through social contacts, decisions usually are
those of the superintendent, although the board does not
support him blindly.

Most research by students of leadership has focused on
two contrasting styles, one labeled as directive or task-oriented, and the other as democratic or group-oriented, with
high consideration for the needs of the individual. Experiments comparing the performance of both types of leaders
have indicated that each is successful in some situations and
not in others. For instance, task orientation may be more
appropriate for a submarine commander than for a college
president. No one has been able to show conclusively that one
kind of leader is always superior or more effective. In the
educational enterprise where suspicion of administration is
rampant, one would expect task-oriented leaders to mask their
hard-driving style by involving others in the process of decision-making in order to coopt support.

We have attempted not to stress in our discussion that

one superintendency style was more desirable than another. Instead we have consistently maintained that the environment (i.e., community power structure and type of board) prescribes the parameters. The main implication we have stressed is that the school system and its supporting community are as responsible for a superintendent's success or failure as he is himself.

The decision-making superintendent is commonly found in rural school districts. One such place in our sample had a school population of about 1,100 students, housed in one large building. The present facility was overcrowded, but a site for a new building had recently been acquired.

The community had one fair-sized industry which produced small boats plus several small plants, including a corset factory. Agriculture remained an important industry, although large and prosperous farms were not in evidence. At the moment, the town center is isolated, both culturally and physically, from large metropolitan areas.

There is a genuine lack of activity in the community, an inertness that signifies more than tacit agreement with what goes on. It has to do with a general lack of community consciousness and cohesion. The editor of the newspaper pointed out, for instance, that there is very little socializing done in the town among the more influential people. They all know each other, of course, but it doesn't seem to occur to them that they might have problems in common.

The school board, while it shows some interest in its responsibilities, it is not vitally involved in school affairs. For one thing it is happy with the way things are going, and it does not want to move ahead too fast: the tax levy is not

even up to the state minimum. The board sees its job as handling personnel problems, kids in trouble, and similar routine
matters.

The superintendent is forced into the decision-making
role almost against his will. His capability, though, has enabled him to handle the position in good fashion. He is
perfectly conscious of his role, and even identified it himself
from the model, but his attitude toward it is professional and
he is not out to grab power. He is anxious to bring things
together so that he can assume a role as professional advisor.
While he thinks that factions may emerge over the building of
the new school, he would prefer that to complete lack of
discussion.

The superintendent described his role modestly but accurately:

> *Interviewer:* How do you conduct yourself at board
> meetings?
> *Superintendent:* I don't keep quiet. I try to be objective.
> The nicest compliment I have had recently was when I
> met one of the board members at the Science Fair and
> he said to me, "Fred, I can't tell which way you want us
> to go." Then I said, 'Well, I did a pretty good job.' When
> it comes down to something that I feel is administrative
> policy or action I make the action and I explain it.
> *Interviewer:* Do they usually seek or take your advice
> on issues?
> *Superintendent:* Yes.
> *Interviewer:* Do they tend to follow you?
> *Superintendent:* Not without question. I come in, I
> hope, quite well prepared on any of these things with as
> much background as I can possibly get.

It goes without saying that in many rural communities,

the superintendent is one of the best-educated men around and his expertise in the teaching arena usually goes relatively unchallenged if, and this is an important if, he appears to have his feet on the ground.

Certainly community passivity leaves the superintendent free to work on educational problems, but then he may miss the creative aspect of tension which comes in communities where external pressures are manifest. In the community just cited, the superintendent identified his main problem as having to "raise the aspiration level of the people in this community as to what the values of education are."

PART SIX

PROFILES OF POWER
AND RECOMMENDATIONS
FOR POLICY

The intent of the authors in the preceding chapters was to provide insight into empirical situations that were either observed by us or reported by our informants. The processes of power relations and conflict seemed to us to fit well into the model outlined in the first chapter. We feel that continued research in the area of power structures would benefit by further testing and modification of the model, for, right or wrong, it does answer some of the fundamental questions in the field. In this interest, our findings are summarized statistically with respect to the fifty-one communities studied in Chapter 11. These statistical findings, based on the classification of communities by judges (see Appendix A), indicate that the relationships posited by the model are confirmed, but imperfectly.

Few people could emerge from research in a large number of communities and the voluminous literature on power and policy relationships in education without being motivated to suggest some changes in the present system. Therefore, we are offering a number of reflections on local control and on what might be done to improve the present system.

Any effort to restructure the status quo in education faces great opposition just in obtaining the necessary public and political acceptance. We do not discount the difficulty of this task. Whether these recommendations are heeded or not, all will not be lost. Anything that informs the public about its local institutions is a gain—the educational enterprise is viable.

11

TESTING
THE MODEL

Our intent in these chapters is not confined to furthering insights into power and conflict solely for the benefit of citizens and educational leaders, but future researchers, too, we hope shall find this model useful. It is also hoped that the quoted material and conclusions drawn will aid research in areas other than school-community relations.

Of utmost importance is the "fit" between the model and the classification of examples. Those judging had available to them material from interviews in addition to that reported in the preceding pages. It is important to point out that in the analysis to follow every attempt was made to obtain valid and reasonably precise findings. The application of statistical formulae to case material is not often attempted by behavioral scientists, but there is no inherent reason why such an integration should not be attempted.

Caution is essential when the literature concerning power structures is interpreted. Power relationships are complex and hard to measure objectively. The lack of comparative studies may be largely due to the unusually difficult methodological and logistical problems involved; it is easier to conduct an intensive case study in which startling descriptive and often entertaining data may be imaginatively analyzed. Small wonder that researchers in this field spend a great deal of time criticizing each other's methods and findings.

HYPOTHESES

Twelve specific directional hypotheses have been derived from the model.

1. A dominated community power structure is most often accompanied by a dominated school board.

2. A factional community power structure is most often accompanied by a factional school board.

3. A pluralistic community power structure is most often accompanied by a status congruent school board.

4. An inert community power structure is most often accompanied by a sanctioning school board.

5. A dominated school board is most often accompanied by the role of functionary being played by the superintendent.

6. A factional school board is most often accompanied by the role of political strategist being played by the superintendent.

7. A status congruent school board is most often accompanied by the role of professional adviser being played by the superintendent.

8. A sanctioning school board is most often accompanied by the role of decision-maker being played by the superintendent.

9. A dominated community power structure is most often accompanied by a role of functionary being played by the superintendent.

10. A factional community power structure is most often accompanied by a role of political strategist being played by the superintendent.

11. A pluralistic community power structure is most often accompanied by a role of professional adviser being played by the superintendent.

12. An inert community power structure is most often accompanied by a role of decision-maker being played by the superintendent.

The first four research hypotheses were designed to test the extent of the association between varying types of community power structures and the classifications of school boards as predicted by the model. Table 1 shows that hypotheses 1 through 4 were confirmed.

In summarizing the relationship between the community power structure and the structure of the school board, it is important to note that a diagonal was theoretically expected on the basis of the model. In Table 1, the dominated community power structure was expected to be followed by a dominated board, a factional power structure by a factional board, and the like.

The highest correlations were to be expected between the structure of the school board and the role of the superintendent. Here the social relationship is formally defined and interactions are frequent and intense.

TABLE 1

RELATIONSHIP OF COMMUNITY POWER STRUCTURE
TO STRUCTURE OF SCHOOL BOARD

School Board Structure

COMMUNITY POWER STRUCTURE	Dominated	Factional	Status Congruent	Sanctioning	Total
Dominated	5	1	1	1	8
Factional	0	6	0	1	7
Pluralistic	2	2	18	1	23
Inert	1	1	3	8	13
Total	8	10	22	11	51

Chi Square = 45.513
P < .001
Phi = .54

Table 2 indicates that hypotheses 5 through 8 were confirmed. The diagonals which were predicted by the model are clearly the cells most frequented. There is less scatter than found in the previous table in which the correlation between the community power structure and the structure of the school board was tested.

The correlation between the community power structure and the role of the superintendent was expected to be lower than either of the two associations. There are several reasons for this. In the first place, the community more often expresses its control over the superintendent through the school board, although this is not exclusively the case. Secondly, there is more room for the power of the community to be contested or at least to fail to be expressed in school decision-making

TABLE 2

RELATIONSHIP OF STRUCTURE OF SCHOOL
BOARD TO ROLE OF SUPERINTENDENT

STRUCTURE OF SCHOOL BOARD	*Role of Superintendent*				
	Functionary	Political Strategist	Professional Adviser	Decision Maker	Total
Dominated	6	0	2	0	8
Factional	1	6	3	0	10
Status Congruent	1	3	16	2	22
Sanctioning	0	0	0	11	11
Total	8	9	21	13	51

Chi Square = 76.89
P < .001
Phi = .71

when there is an intermediary role, namely that of the board member. In other words, the social distance is greater, and the room for error in implementing power is greater.

On the other hand, there is some direct control by power figures in the community over the superintendent. This is expressed, as we found in the study, through personal associations, through clubs, and through the desire of the superintendent sometimes to preempt the legal functioning of the board to protect himself. Furthermore, the correlations between the community structure and the structure of the board, as well as those between the structure of the board and role of the superintendent, should, logically, produce some correlation between the community power structure and the role of the superintendent.

The ninth hypothesis states that a dominated community power structure would more often be associated with the functionary role in the office of the superintendent. For the first time, less than a majority of the cases corresponds to the expected pattern on the basis of the model (see Table 3). Only three of eight cases followed this hypothesis, while five superintendents in dominated communities played roles other than that expected on the basis of the model.

This calls into question the wording of the hypotheses we set out to study. What does the term "more often associated with" mean? Do we mean a numerical majority, or do we mean simply the most frequent association? Since the model indicates that a numerical majority of cases should follow the expected pattern, we must reject this hypothesis.

Table 3 demonstrates that hypotheses 10 through 12 were confirmed. It is apparent that the correlation between

TABLE 3

RELATIONSHIP OF COMMUNITY POWER STRUCTURE
TO ROLE OF SUPERINTENDENT

| COMMUNITY STRUCTURE | *Role of Superintendent* | | | | |
	Functionary	Political Strategist	Professional Adviser	Decision Maker	Total
Dominated	3	1	2	2	8
Factional	0	4	2	1	7
Pluralistic	4	3	14	2	23
Inert	1	1	3	8	13
Total	8	9	21	13	51

the community structure and the role of the superintendent is the lowest of the three basic correlations.

The relationships posited by the model were found to hold in most cases, although not perfectly. Further, our data indicate that it is possible to identify and categorize types of power structure, school board structure, and administrative style on the basis of relatively few interviews taken by a team in a short time.

NEEDS FOR FURTHER RESEARCH

Other than the work of Jennings,[1] who employed a different research methodology than Hunter, little original research in patterns of community power has been reported, and there appears to be little recognition that several different typologies of power structure may exist, or that communities may often be characterized in transition from one type of structure to another. A related problem involves classification within the typologies. For example, what is the difference in terms of associations within the community political system between weak and vigorous pluralism or irregular and constant dominance by an elite? Furthermore, although to study power is certainly to study decision-making, studies generally fail to reflect satisfactory decision-making models applicable to the types of power patterns revealed.

The fact that a large number of previous studies would fit into the typology of community power structures of the model herein used indicates that the general character of the model needs further testing and refinement in larger studies. Relatively clear evidence of dominated power structures occurs in various studies, including those by Lynds,[2] Hunter,[3] D'Antonio and Erickson,[4] D'Antonio, Form, Loomis, and Erickson,[5] and others.[6]

A number of studies, usually of more than one community, is also available on factional structures; these include work by Gamson,[7] Minar,[8] Coleman,[9] and Malone.[10] In the main these are studies of conflict in situations where there is not an institutionalized system for airing severe disagreements short of painful and emotionally costly attacks on persons and institutions. Several studies have been referred to previously on the pluralistic community, including those by Dahl,[11] and Polsby,[12] and there are also those by Mills, Davis [13] and Banfield.[14]

The few studies of inert communities may be due to the greater conceptual interest shown the related subjects of alienation and apathy. It can be argued, however, that in the main the findings of Vidich and Bensman indicate at least a community helplessness, if not the failure of power figures to develop a recognizable structure.[15] Where power is separated by institution, Sanders and Ensminger have shown communities in which the power figures exert leadership in economic affairs to the exclusion of every other problem area.[16]

In addition to further testing the model we have used, it would be of critical importance to determine the effect of patterns not predicted by this model. For example, we already have some evidence that superintendents whose role playing does not fit the expected pattern, e.g. a decision-maker in a factional board and community, have but brief tenure. It may also be the case that a mixture between community and board types, such as a dominated community and factional board, results in involuntary resignation on the part of the superintendent, regardless of the role he plays. The average tenure of the superintendent in the United States is 3.7 years, hardly a satisfactory basis for the chief administrator of such an important agency. Such brief tenure hardly encourages long range plans, experimental programs which may fail, or leadership on controversial issues.

Changes in structure are most interesting. We believe the research of others indicates that dominated power is weakest when issues are brought to a vote. The effect of "defeat" on the subsequent effectiveness of the dominators is not known.

Within the same problem area, the increasing activism of women in bond issues, election campaigns, and in education of the public may bring about, we suspect, a tendency toward the pluralistic system. Research on the dynamics of this situation is of increasing importance. Many housewives have the intelligence and talent to be power figures themselves if they were to become directly involved in the labor force; their willingness to devote their available time to community development may greatly change the structure of communities and community-wide boards.

The educational issues surrounding desegregation have brought many dominators out of hiding, have spurred many previously inactive people into attempts to wield power, and have produced factional communities from all three other types. Whether "rancorous" conflict can resolve issues, and whether it can be allayed to allow other approaches to subsequent problems is deserving of our most careful attention.

As a philosophy of confrontation filters down from universities and colleges to high school students we may see entirely new factions and interest groups appearing on the community scene. Ascribed and achieved status are both on the side of the adults, but youth also has its weapons. Add to the new factions created by youth the advent of teachers who stand up to be counted and we may have types of power and conflict not envisioned in the model offered herein nor by previous students of community relations.

And last, there are conflicts in American society inherent in state and local levels of control, especially now that the federal government is entering this domain in significant ways. The effects of such a powerful but distant adversary entering the fray are not known, but the hypotheses suggested by persons of different political persuasions and from different regions of the country are hardly the cold, analytical, emotion-free propositions we read about in methods texts.

NOTES

1. M. Kent Jennings, *Community Influentials: The Elites of Atlanta,* New York: Free Press of Glencoe, 1964.
2. Robert S. Lynd and Helen M. Lynd, *Middletown in Transition,* New York: Harcourt, Brace, and Co., 1937.
3. Floyd Hunter, *Community Power Structure,* Chapel Hill: University of North Carolina Press, 1953.
4. William V. D'Antonio and Eugene C. Erickson, "The Reputational Technique as a Measure of Community Power: An Evaluation Based on Comparative and Longitudinal Studies," *American Sociological Review* 27, June, 1962, pp. 362–376.
5. William V. D'Antonio, William H. Form, Charles P.

Loomis, and Eugene Erickson, "Institutional and Occupational Representations in Eleven Community Influence Systems," *American Sociological Review* 26, June, 1961, pp. 440–446.

6. For a compilation of such studies, see William V. D'Antonio and H. J. Ehrlich, editors, *Power and Democracy in America,* Notre Dame, Ind.: University of Notre Dame Press, 1961.

7. William A. Gamson, "Rancorous Conflict in Community Politics," *American Sociological Review* 31, February, 1966, pp. 71–81.

8. David W. Minar, "The Community Basis of Conflict in School System Politics," *American Sociological Review* 31, December, 1966, pp 822–835.

9. James S. Coleman, *Community Conflict,* Glencoe, Illinois: The Free Press, 1957.

10. Joseph F. Malone, "The Lonesome Train in Levittown," *The Inter-University Case Program, Revised Edition,* Tuscaloosa, Alabama: The University of Alabama Press, 1958.

11. Robert A. Dahl, *Who Governs?,* New Haven: Yale University Press, 1961.

12. Nelson W. Polsby, *Community Power and Political Theory,* New Haven: Yale University Press, 1963.

13. Warner E. Mills, Jr. and Harry R. Davis, *Small City Government: Seven Cases in Decision Making,* New York: Random House, 1962.

14. Edward C. Banfield, *Big City Politics,* New York: Random House, 1965. Banfield also includes cities which, from his analysis, appear to be factional.

15. Arthur J. Vidich and Joseph Bensman, *Smalltown in Mass Society: Class, Power, and Religion in a Rural Community,* Princeton: Princeton University Press, 1958.

16. Irwin T. Sanders and Douglas Ensminger, "Alabama Rural Communities: A Study of Chilton County," *Alabama College Bulletin* 136, Montevallo, Alabama, 1940.

12

REFLECTIONS
ON POLICY

This study was designed to test empirically the strength of what we consider to be an analytically useful model. Power and authority at the local community level are complex, problematic issues; administrative techniques are frequently hopelessly dated, and the competence of many board members and school administrators open to serious question. Power structures in American communities are fluid, ever changing in composition, and difficult to classify. For example, a dominated community may be imperceptibly moving toward factionalism, although dominants may still be able to control the important decisions. Researchers who opt to study the community at some subsequent point in time might find a factional situation. Considering the present rate of social change, such a discovery would be more probable than improbable.

If we were to indulge in the current fashion for predicting the state of the future, we would not join those who foresee the early demise of local government. It is true that we live in a world increasingly dominated by man-made machines and systems. The continued deterioration of the environment caused by poorly-designed systems, processes, and machines must be halted and reversed or we shall all face oblivion. Hopefully, a new art in policy-making and planning procedures will be devised to shape, direct, and regulate technological change as we move toward systems of even greater complexity. Large metropolitan centers embracing inner cities and suburban communities are expected to eventually submerge the highly personalized and parochial village or town, now memorialized as the backbone of the American spirit of individualism and personal freedom. Superior financial resources have already enabled state governments to steadily encroach on the tasks formerly reserved for the local community; in certain areas, and for the same reason, the federal government intrudes as well.

For the foreseeable future, however, local community control will remain a powerful force. By such mechanisms as failing to comply in toto with the regulations promulgated, refusing help outright, interpreting statutes to fit local preferences, using delaying tactics, and the like, community power structures have resiliently warded off the effects of many externally imposed strictures on their freedoms. What makes local control so appealing is the simple fact that it is directly accountable to the people. Whether it uses its power wisely, of course, is another matter. While the property tax continues as an important revenue producer, and there is no indication that it will be replaced, local power structures will continue to exert power in vital political areas. Education, with its heavy dependence on local revenues, is certainly one of these areas.

Critics who insist that power structures are more ephemeral than real do have a point. Power potential is not the same as the use of power; neither do power-wielders decide every issue that comes along. We may be almost convinced that robber barons are relics of the past until we read that Henry Ford actually does run the Ford Motor Company, or that beer lobbies in Wisconsin are able to keep beer taxes low. What better examples do we need to prove the existence of power groups?

Is the ordinary citizen impotent in the exercise of local government? Does the existence of some form of power structure represent a repudiation of representative democracy? As any practicing political figure knows, the constituent always has the last word if he chooses to exercise it. Most of the time, by silent consent, he permits himself to be governed by others. Occasionally, he becomes exercised over an issue and joins hands with like-minded colleagues to register his protest. Any power structure will listen carefully to the rumblings of the body politic in order not to be humbled in a public confrontation.

The control exercised by power structures is sometimes tenuous, temporary, and limited in application, but generally it is not. One may search in vain in some communities for the combination of forces needed to carry through a project and find nothing but inertia. Elsewhere, local officialdom may be so obdurate in interpreting statutes that decision-making is hopelessly entangled in red tape; civil servants, in short, can dominate simply by virtue of occupying rule-ridden bureaucratic positions in local government.

Today, individuals previously without power are rapidly becoming aware of the strength that can be marshalled if they work together. Local community action groups are certainly much more knowledgeable in the areas of political strategy and pressures than they used to be.

Local communities are well described as political organisms striving to achieve a viable mechanism acceptable to the constituency involved for deciding controversial issues, and that underlying this process is a political power structure of some kind.

Theorists over the years have been proclaiming the death knell of local school boards; yet they are still very much alive and show no signs of disappearing. Their usefulness has often been questioned on the grounds that amateurs, no matter how gifted, are ill prepared to pass judgment on technical educational matters such as curriculum, teacher evaluation, and organizational innovations. In order to justify their existence, boards have supposedly spent their energy supervising budgets and bond issues, while protecting the community against the invasion of unpopular ideas. If peace and tranquility reign, the board usually rubber stamps the recommendations of the administrator, reserving its prerogative to watch over the tax rate. If conflict erupts the board is often tempted to assuage public opinion by taking over active management of school affairs. The analogy between public schools and higher educational institutions is instructive here. Student riots have energized boards of trustees and challenged the hallowed principle of academic freedom. The California

episodes during the reign of Governor Ronald Reagan under-
scored this point. Some riots, of course, have moved school
and university boards to take constructive action and to increase the quality of their knowledge base.

The above description is not intended as a caricature.
Most school districts have been small enough for a school
board to monitor activities down to the classroom behavior of
a particular teacher, control mechanisms that have been
somewhat restricted by the rapid growth in the size of school
districts.

Still, a cursory reading of the daily newspaper will
reveal that the situation has not changed much. An Arizona
school system may fingerprint its teachers and the State of
California may require the Biblical interpretation of Genesis
in its science textbooks.

The greatest blow to board independence has been dealt
by the phenomenal growth of militant teacher unions that
come armed with highly developed bargaining techniques
along with a willingness and even eagerness to strike. The
self-effacing teacher has been replaced by an aggressive, acti-
vist-oriented one. Once grievance procedures are mandated
by law, no teacher protected by tenure need worry about
expressing controversial viewpoints in the classroom. Is it
possible that teacher power has rendered obsolete the old
forms of control we have gone to some lengths to describe?
Our answer is an emphatic no.

While it is no secret that boards are not overjoyed with
the prospect of spending long hours in negotiating sessions
with teacher-bargaining units, in due time the most onerous
part of this work will be taken over by the board's own set
of labor negotiators. Boards will adapt to the new circum-

stances with some unhappiness but their ultimate control over the educational process, though diluted, will still be considerable.

In fact, the tensions so apparent throughout American society have galvanized boards into the political arena with a vengeance. The New York State School Boards Association has gone on record as favoring the abolition of tenure laws for teachers. Confrontation has become a way of life and dissidents of many persuasions are demanding that boards use their influence to satisfy their expectations. Boards are products of the community they represent; if under heavy pressure from constituents they will normally respond in terms of the parameters permitted them. In the pluralistic community, the board member may still be provided the luxury of deciding policy in terms of his own persuasion. The board member in a factional community cannot take a position in opposition to the group he represents, unless, of course, he is prepared to endanger the probability of reelection or reappointment. Somehow such a board member has to survive by balancing competing forces and keeping the opposition off balance.

The time when school board members remained aloof from the day-to-day travail, arousing themselves only for ceremonial occasions, is long since past. Board members are now vulnerable political servants, not honored custodians of the public weal. Their advantage, of course, is that they occupy a part-time role, and defeat does not mean the end of a career, in the professional sense. To the extent that board members have their eyes on political advancement they are likely to test the prevailing currents among their constituency. Though not a heroic stance, behavior of this sort is more realistic than cynical. The prospect is that boards are in for a hard time; the buffer role between the public and the professional school personnel is nettlesome, indeed, particularly when society is unsettled and insecure.

The public is fickle and uninformed; this statement succinctly describes the ordinary political environment which the educational administrator accepts either at the visceral level or, more hopefully, from intellectual understanding. Industry has called the foreman the "man in the middle"; by contrast, his role is so well defined and restricted in scope compared to that of the superintendent of schools, that we need to invent new terminology if we want to draw a useful analogy. The head football coach faces some of the same difficult questions with a more simplistic charge; the top business executive, though expected to produce profits, is immune from public clamor unless he makes a colossal blunder, and even the tragedy of this error may be overcome if he controls the exchequer. While the Edsel car is humorously referred to as a magnificent failure, Mr. Ford himself survived, and even more amazing, Robert McNamara did too.

The superintendent is restricted in his acts of leadership by the nature of the power structure in the community which he serves. On an immediate level, he is subject to the vagaries of his direct superiors, the board of education. A recent quotation from the press eloquently poses the problem:

> So why should the superintendent be exposed to being undone by a bunch of bush league board members who just happened to be on the right ticket in the right election? . . . . We would not appoint a baseball manager to run the team and then name a committee of bleacher experts to keep him from following his own judgement (Detroit *Free Press,* Wednesday, October 8, 1969).

In this particular instance the news media was commenting on the well-publicized resignation of the state superintendent of public instruction in Michigan under duress from a politically elected and divided state board of education From Governor William G. Milliken of Michigan came this strong statement in support of the superintendent:

> Dr. Ira Polley, by his resignation, has shown himself, again, to be a man of great courage and integrity. Although I am deeply sorry to see him leave his position as Superintendent of Public Instruction, I respect his decision in light of the intolerable conditions under which he has been forced to function. Dr. Polley has worked hard for education in Michigan, and all of us owe him a great debt of gratitude for serving with distinction and dedication under difficult and distracting circumstances (Detroit *Free Press,* Monday, October 6, 1969).

Can an administrator act as a professional advisor if he is reporting to a factional board? A superintendent might, of course, put on a public show of indignation and denounce his board of education. Taking the issue to the public makes banner headlines; visible action may be perceived as evidence of strong "leadership." But would it bring results?

There is little in the recent literature of public administration to suggest that it would. Usually, school administrators feel that open battle is futile. In any event, defiant theatrics have their counterproductive tendencies and the school system is certain to suffer. It appears that when the superintendent and his board of education are out of step, there is little that can be done about it.

Abetting this power disequilibrium is the public's lack of confidence in the professional educator's wisdom, a disenchantment commonly referred to as a credibility gap. Public opinion wavers between support for an elite or an egalitarian school system; between the neighborhood school and forced integration bussing; between sex education as a school function and sex education as a family responsibility. Caught in the middle of these value conflicts is the superintendent of schools.

Like professionals of any persuasion school administrators are heavily influenced by their occupational organizations, such as the American Association of School Administrators, and the colleges of education in which they received their basic preparation. The doctrine propounded from these sources may not square with the values and objectives held by nonprofessional board members and ordinary citizens who think differently and use a different universe of discourse.

Complicating the affair is the fact that educational theorists do not themselves agree on many of the fundamental issues undergirding the teaching process. A classic example is the extended controversy over learning theory. Is learning the adding together of originally independent elements, or the blind reinforcement or inhibition of particular response tendencies, or is it a reorganization of a psychological field? The competing camps into which the experts are divided has only added to the public's confusion. The public debates held by reading specialists expounding the case of phonics versus word recognition is another area of disagreement that further erodes the confidence of the lay person; he questions whether there is a science of education. If teaching is an art, then selection rather than training becomes the crucial ingredient. These factors all tend to fracture the leadership potential of the superintendent of schools.

In his own defense it must be admitted that the superintendent has not received the kind of training that will best equip him for the management job he will actually confront. At best the board member regards the superintendent as a valued advisor; at worst he is viewed as an obstructionist or defensive scapegoat, with an undertone of suspicion concerning his ability to administer. In short, the employer-employee relationship is a source of substantial pressure on the superintendent.

There certainly is no indication that this fragile relationship will be improved in the immediate future. The intransigence of teacher unions and the increased intensity of student rebellion presage more rather than less tension between superintendents and school boards.

RECOMMENDATIONS

Recommendations about how to improve local governmental decision-making in the field of education keep turning up with depressing regularity. Many of the soothsayers do not hesitate to offer grandiose schemes for change with a remarkably thin knowledge base. Our study revealed numerous deviations from ideal behavior; grievous faults and hypocrisies involving the whole fabric of modern society appeared. Like other researchers we uncovered some unpleasantries about communities, at the same time we were having to deal with school bureaucracies staffed by experts who were unyielding, dogmatic, and short-sighted. Theirs was a different kind of narrowness.

How does one approach the task of developing a viable

set of solutions to the problems we encountered? If one chooses to draw up a list of apocalyptic new ideas, political realism dictates that the impact is apt to be minimal in practice although these ideas may strike a chord of responsiveness at the intellectual level. The early demise of most blue-ribbon task force reports is mute testimony in an often repeated phenomenon. To depict an abstractly better system that will never see the light of day is not a very rewarding endeavor.

The decision to suggest incremental modifications, on the other hand, often falls victim to the curse of banality. The moderate critic, who thinks the system needs widespread reform but can be salvaged, sounds like the unromantic voice of the establishment. For example, the perennial recommendation that small school systems should be consolidated into larger units is safe, conventional, and acceptable, but is it worth repeating once more?

Conventional wisdom prescribes that the board-superintendent relationship must be based not only on external forms but also on the inner spirit of the democratic principle; in essence, both parties must be mutually respectful of each other's positions. It logically follows that an educational program will flourish only when it is led by both an effective board and an effective executive who are able to work together cooperatively. The board-superintendent relationship can never be completely free of tension but it should be free of personal aggrandizement, demagoguery, and political grandstanding.

A traditional nonrevolutionary reform for reaching this objective might be to suggest that boards of education should provide their chief executives with a reasonable form of term contract, perhaps three to five years, renewable annually.

This provides for an annual audit of the superintendent's performance, and lessens the critical short-range emphasis by the superintendent on establishing good will with his employers as the surest method to continued tenure.

Few would deny the merits of this eminently sensible plan. Variations on this theme might be added. Would it not be helpful if board members and the superintendent sat down at least once a year for a frank and open discussion (in private, of course) in which each party to the contract might state how he felt about how the partnership was evolving. If it accomplished nothing more, it might prove a useful therapeutic measure. Another step, a little more dramatic, is to suggest that board members and their superintendent attend a sensitivity training session where outside specialists take over the responsibility for developing mutual awareness.

We submit that these reasonable ideas while worthy of consideration would do little to change present structural arrangements. The chief cause underlying much of the disaffection between boards and superintendents is the unequalities of their power relationship. Board controls and checks, in theory, law, and practice, are overwhelming. The board is clearly the dominant partner. Why? The board selects the executive, prescribes his conditions of work, and if it wishes, may replace him. The board needs to recognize this controlling relationship and avoid arbitrary exercise of authority over its superintendent; the superintendent should not be a broker trading in the pressures and demands of community conflict.

One way to equalize the power discrepancy would be to prescribe that the state department of education be charged with the responsibility of appointing all local superintendents of schools. Corporations, the armed forces, and established churches all use this technique. Though appointed by an outside authority the administrator would not be free to completely ignore the wishes of the local constituency. Complaints about his performance could be transmitted to the central authority and redress achieved. This procedure enables an administrator to be judged on the basis of his performance and provides him with more leverage to change the system. Since education is a state function, what better way to place the responsibility for the quality of schools where it belongs?

On the other hand, it would be interesting to take a systems analysis point of view and redesign the entire educational enterprise.

In order that we may appeal to a variety of readers we propose some basic recommendations which might be termed useful improvements in the present system, and others that suggest modifications and reorganizations in our institutions. We shall not attempt to build a theoretically ideal system.

These recommendations are neither original nor exhaustive, but we believe they merit serious consideration by individuals interested in improving education.

For the Superintendent

1. *Principal effort should be placed on developing important educational issues instead of concentrating on the endless administrative details.*

A day in the life of the average school superintendent is as tightly controlled as a fixed agenda. There are so many reports to read, people to see, committee meetings to attend, speeches to write, budget decisions to make, and the like, that the superintendent's mind is shattered and inundated by the sheer quantity and variety of demands placed upon it. Unfortunately, the tendency is to react to these multiple pressures rather than to select tasks along a quality dimension. The superintendent needs to change his habits of mind and try to build rather than follow public preferences. It is he who should be clarifying what good education is all about.

2. *The superintendent should systematically build a political base inside and outside his school system; he should legitimize programs ahead of time.*

Any administrator has to guard against the structural insulation inherent in hierarchical organizations. A superintendent is probably most comfortable with his own administrative staff (i.e., his assistant superintendents, staff assistants, and building principals). If he deals almost exclusively with this group, his own points of view are certain to be systematically reinforced since he is the titular leader. Strenuous efforts are required to interact directly with teacher groups in order that reality testing can take place. The larger the size of the organization the more likely the superintendent may become a remote, ceremonial, and distant figure, a splendid isolation he cannot afford.

With his own staff the superintendent builds support by the clear delegation of tasks which utilize as fully as possible the individual abilities of his administrative colleagues. Able professionals are not attracted to superintendents who severely circumscribe a subordinate administrator's opportunity for growth and development by retaining most of the power and prestige for themselves. The responsibility, of course, rightfully rests on the superintendent.

If the superintendent is to speak forcefully on educational issues publicly, as we have recommended, he needs to acquire an enduring, steady political constituency. It is not enough for the administrator to talk, he needs to be influential in forming public opinion on educational issues. While intuition plays an important role, there are all sorts of pragmatic steps which can be taken without compromising principles. The superintendent should meet and talk with all major public political figures in the community, and establish contacts with state and federal governmental officials, particularly those representing his constituency. Opinion surveys, analysis of election results, participation and membership in important community groups, attendance at key community meetings, and other methods designed to feel the pulse of the community should be undertaken. These responsibilities cannot be fully delegated to others; the superintendent speaks for the system and unless he is a romantic in the Eugene McCarthy mold, he must lay a firm basis for accomplishing the goals he articulates. Without a personal political base the superintendent has to seek safety in blandness or face constant job insecurity.

3. The superintendent should symbolize both by intellect and will his own humanity.

We find it particularly disturbing and ironic that the modern-day administrator is often cast in the role of a knownothing. It is not expected that he display those attributes associated with the man who enjoys dialogue about ideas as ideas, who displays a lively curiosity and a fertile imagination, and who is comfortable in the company of men of all seasons.

The superintendent has to administer himself as a person as well as his organization. He needs regular exercise, adequate vacations, stimulating experiences, time for contem-

plation, and the opportunity to read voraciously in a variety
of fields. He has to join the knowledge explosion. It is tragic
to observe administrators who are so harried by the pressure
of daily decision-making that they develop a resistance, probably unintentional, to the processes of inquiry which stamp a
man as truly educated.

4. *The superintendent should consciously attempt to build a
favorable leadership image.*

Is it style or circumstance? We have argued throughout
that circumstance is a significant factor; our model posits behavioral relationships between environmental constraints and
administrative action. What is possible in any given situation
depends to some extent on the material resources at the administrator's disposal. No one would be so foolish, however,
to discount the possibility that there are individuals able to
surmount difficult circumstances and succeed. Building an
image implies exposure; many a technically proficient administrator has been summarily deposed because he was
fundamentally an unknown. Charismatics, like Max Rafferty,
may be unpopular with the professional fraternity, but they
carry an undisputed magic with the public citizenry. If an
issue is explosive enough, the administrator must declare his
position, and if he has failed to project a proper image, he is
certain to face the wrath of the disaffected. By *proper* we
do not mean an undefinable virtue existing in any particular
man but that a degree of image consciousness is required. The
man who is scrupulously honest, fair, forceful, sophisticated,
and courageous needs to make these qualities known to
others. If he allows himself to become a faceless front for an
impervious school bureaucracy, he shall suffer the indignities

befitting such ignominity. Image-making, in short, may enable the administrator to give his community a few injections of change even if his political support is shaky.

5. *Superintendents should learn how to be master administrators; in this instance we are referring to ordering processes in such a way that means are appropriate to ends.*

Even a cursory study of school superintendents leads one to conclude that good management practices are frequently lacking. Visits to small school systems which tend to employ relatively inexperienced or poorly trained men, and meetings with school administrators unskilled in administrative behavior—their training primarily from books and devoid of apprenticeship opportunities—contribute to this poor impression.

The superintendent needs a good secretary and a good deputy, and he needs to know how to use them effectively. Further, he has to learn to delegate most operational functions to others. He should reserve for himself those tasks likely to make a difference over the long term and concentrate his energies in areas where his special talents enable him to be most productive. The inexperienced administrator is likely to shrink from making decisions which will tend to irritate people in the short run; the experienced administrator quickly senses that a man is ultimately judged not by one decision but by the cumulative effect of many. Educational administrators could profit from attending some of the workshops and clinics held by the American Management Association and the AASA National Academy for School Executives where emphasis is placed on learning management skills as well as theoretical constructs. While adminis-

shun

trators need to theorize, they cannot afford to eschew day-to-day management responsibilities.

6. *Since the quality of education depends on the talents of individual teachers, the superintendent should give much more attention to the selection process.*

We are not suggesting that the superintendent should himself interview every prospective new teacher (if the school system is small enough, it is not such a bad idea), but rather that he should be intimately involved in working out suitable policies and procedures that would guarantee high standards. Selection of teachers is an example of an activity having a highly significant effect on the future of the organization; it should never become a routine processing affair. He must have the knack for sensing whether new staff members are high quality or not.

7. *Like any political leader, a superintendent of schools should be ready to resign whenever necessary to advance the cause of education in the school system under his charge.*

Once an impasse has developed in a community over a vital educational issue and the superintendent has been instrumental in advancing a position that has been repudiated by the body politic, the correct action is to seek a position elsewhere. We are not suggesting that superintendents be masochistic and withdraw at the earliest indication of dissent, but that an educational leader cannot function without minimal acceptance. There is much to be said for the idea of voluntary rotation which is often practiced by the best superintendents; a change at the top every five to seven years may help regenerate a moribund school system.

8. *The superintendent should see himself as the prime advocate of educational innovations.*

We think that an educational statesman should lead not follow. It is he who should be recommending differentiated staffing, personalized instruction, more extensive use of media, and the like, rather than waiting for pressures to build from his constituency. The education he may have to give to his board, his staff, and his community is an uncommonly fine art. He wisely may not agree that all the new modes of instruction are valuable, in which case he should marshal evidence and arguments for alternative techniques. In sum, it is his duty to recommend policy and back these positions with scrupulous data.

We are opposed to the frequently expressed idea that superintendents should think of themselves as teachers in the sense of never leaving the classroom, or of being master teachers able to personally direct the teaching process of every classroom in the district. The superintendent cannot afford this indulgence; he is not a teacher's teacher, rather he should be an administrator's administrator.

9. *The superintendent who wishes to influence curricular change must find the techniques that will permit him to fruitfully engage faculty and students in the planning process.*

Too much planning in education is done from the top. Sometimes the ill effects of this grand design schema are moderated by cooptative mechanisms, as when faculty committees, chaired and subtly controlled by the superintendent or his chief lieutenant, are sold the desired product.

Frequently, when a change has been implanted the main actors (the teachers) sabotage it by refusing to implement it to the fullest. In the past the students were not even considered worthy of consultation.

The era of confrontation has changed the rules of the game. If the superintendent really wants to make substantive changes he must involve representatives from among the teachers and students. Further, these individuals should be chosen early enough so that their contribution is considered in the deliberations. Change will be slower but hopefully it will be more effective.

Fear of teacher-student involvement stems from the immature and narrow self-interest projected by some student activists and some teachers. Involvement in the total process and education on a wide array of problems helps make the immature mature and the self-interested more considerate.

10. *Superintendents should develop their own in-service training sessions and not rely excessively on professional courses randomly offered at colleges and universities.*

For many years in-service training programs for teachers have lacked any tangible results; too frequently the school system has relied on impromptu workshops which import one of the peripatetic experts currently in vogue who delivers an impassioned plea for installing the prevailing fashion in educational innovation. Unfortunately, too much reliance has also been placed on the value of graduate courses not designed or related to system needs. Far better it would be if superintendents would structure their own in-service training programs so that a stated purpose could become the rationale for the program. In this way talented members of the local staff might be utilized and outside experts brought in only when their special knowledge could be used to advantage.

11. *The superintendent should never take himself too seriously; a sense of humor and a tolerance for ambiguity are prerequisites for the position.*

Good mental health is essentially the ingredient we are opting for. Battered by the multiple pressures of managing an enterprise whose goals are inchoate and indefinite, the man at the helm must be able to laugh at his failures and roll with the punches without losing his sense of balance. Few will be impressed if the superintendent tries to evoke sympathy or asks for surcease from his labors; more of his constituents will prefer the happy warrior type even if he is a sterling adversary.

12. *Several systems-oriented changes not requiring complete redesign are in order.*

For example, superintendents might be encouraged to develop mechanisms for more effective coordination on a formal or informal basis with other local and regional public nonschool agencies. Increased emphasis by superintendents on long- and short-range planning activities would seem desirable. Superintendents should be free enough from administrative detail to enable them to devote a substantial portion of their time to important social issues bearing on education such as race, poverty, and general social militancy. Additionally, superintendents might be encouraged to have fewer psychological "hang-ups" if territoriality concepts were applied to school districts. Examination of the interrelationships between school districts and public agencies, and school districts and neighboring school districts and public agencies, and school districts and neighboring school districts should be encouraged. Finally, considerably more delegation of responsibility to building-level administrators seems advisable. Meaningful budgeting and financial control at the building level linked to the educational program would free central office administrators from a considerable amount of detail and might promote more differentiated approaches keyed to meeting the needs of school district constituents.

Boards of Education

1. *Boards of education must make a special effort to develop careful screening processes for the selection of superintendents.*

This critical task has often been a hit-or-miss affair; the administrator resigns, dies, or retires, and the board is faced with a one-time responsibility for which it is generally ill prepared. If the general public and the board are satisfied with the way the schools have been operating, there is a tendency to select someone from within the system whose behavior is predictable and safe. If the system is in a state of turmoil, an outsider is more likely to be chosen. In either case, systematic procedures should be followed to insure that a high-quality administrator is obtained who has the skills needed to cope with the challenges inherent in today's educational milieu. The search should be thorough in scope, rigorous in standards, and specific in responsibilities, with consideration given to candidates of surpassing ability who have demonstrated competence in other walks of life.

2. *Boards of education should take responsibility for supporting the case for good education at all political levels, but particularly for their own school system.*

There is no better raison d'etre for the existence of local

school boards. The attitude of the board member should be to fight for what is right in the educational arena rather than compromise on something that is inadequate but will sell. The board should be strong enough to mobilize public support in times of crisis. Good boardmanship ought to be a free-wheeling and risky enterprise. A statement demanding sacrifice of others is easy to make, but the point still remains that if the board of education does not vigorously advocate quality education and convince the citizenry of its value, then, by default, it has abrogated its responsibility. Ideally, good school board members ought to be ahead of their local communities in their judgments about educational ideas and issues.

3.   *Boards should take the initiative to sponsor open evaluative and review sessions with their superintendents.*

The working relationship between boards and superintendents is much more strained than is usually assumed. We found very few really harmonious situations in which both parties were fully satisfied with their respective roles and responsibilities. There is a real communication gap. If boards established clear-cut annual evaluative procedures for their chief administrator, much misunderstanding might be avoided. Term contracts, renewable annually, provide the mechanism for encouraging this procedure. Boards often fail to give a superintendent notice of his inadequacies until it is too late for him to modify his behavior.

We are not advocating that the administrator should refrain from vigorously administering the school system and become a Pollyanna; the able man is bound to cause some trouble if he tries to do his job well. We are arguing against the tendency of some boards to fail to report to the superintendent when they have some reservations about his performance. No one gains in such a circumstance.

4. *Boards of education have an accountability responsibility which cannot be ignored or avoided.*

Today, the taxpayer is raising a hard question: What am I getting for my money? Trite answers couched in terms of numbers of merit scholarships won, class size, qualifications of teachers available, quality of buildings and equipment provided, ring unconvincingly. People want to know if the students can read, have learned an employable skill, and are ready for college. Performance standards are no more difficult to measure than the subjective marks we have grown accustomed to. Boards need to pioneer in this intriguing aspect of educational evaluation.   CANVAS MAKING POL. SPEACHES

5. *Boards of education should stump for higher salaries, for sabbatical leaves and other perquisites for their superintendents and fellow administrators.*

Unions are geared to negotiate for teachers and non-classified personnel; the administrators are dependent upon the wisdom and generosity of the governing board. While man does not work for bread alone, it is not reasonable to expect able people to assume cardiac posts without sufficient remuneration and other rewards to make it worth the candle. Too many school administrators have adopted the stance of indispensability to the detriment of their own health and the ultimate welfare of the school system. A few weeks' harried vacation in the summer doesn't compensate for the cumulative tensions of an administrative year. It is the board of education who should insist that its administrative corps be well paid and well rested.

6. *Boards of education should educate themselves by extensive reading and attendance at clinics held by their own state association and by the National School Boards Association.*

One does not become a capable school board member by accident. Admittedly, some individuals bring experience to a board that enables them to be productive almost from the onset. However, experienced board members are agreed that it takes about one year, or a full cycle, before one is cognizant of the whole range of responsibilities involved. Learning time can be reduced significantly if the board member avails himself of the innumerable opportunities for attending special programs and clinics especially designed to assist him. Away from the irritations of local issues, the board member can gain new perspectives which may prove to be invaluable in coping with intransigent problems at home.

7. *Boards should take a solemn oath to refrain from usurping the prerogatives of its administrative officer.*

The old canon that boards make policy and that superintendents administer it has rightfully been condemned as an oversimplification. In the ultimate sense, decisions are made by the people who hold the power. Since, legally, the board of education has the power, one might expect it to use its power whenever so motivated. The problem arises when the board reaches down and invades the domain assigned to the administrator, as for example, when boards try to discipline individual teachers for malfeasance in office, acts which should be covered by general policy dictums. Throughout our research, we found repeated examples of breakdowns in the supposed division of labor between board and superintendent. As the holder of power, it is the board who determines the character of the relationship.

8. *Boards of education ought to demand criteria for the employment of the teaching staff.*

The hiring of a teacher is not a perfunctory task. It happens that the exigencies of circumstance often force boards to devote countless hours to matters of finance, building needs, and the like; in this vacuum it is all too easy to give short shrift to personnel policies. Few would dispute the contention that teachers make or break a school system. For this reason, it is imperative that boards develop firm policies setting forth detailed specifications in this crucial area. Occasional participation in interviews of prospective candidates is worthwhile and necessary. What better way for a board member to appreciate the quality of the teacher being inducted into the system?

9. *Board members should make as much use as possible of citizen committees and ad hoc advisory groups on specific problems.*

Minority group demands have long been ignored by boards of education, a situation that is no longer tenable. We know that it is good administrative practice to establish positive linkages with all identifiable points of view within the community so that changing values can be efficiently communicated at the decision-making level. Citizen committees, if representative, are superb devices for achieving this goal.

10. *Boards of education should become more politically responsible.*

There seems to be little reason why boards of education should be apolitical while other public boards are closely identified with particular political parties and particular political party goals. We would recommend that political parties

consider running slates of candidates for school board positions in local communities. This would create an atmosphere
of collective party responsibility for educational programs;
allow the party out of power to project alternative solutions
to problems; increase the clarification of issues; put some
political muscle behind educational programs and educational needs; and would increase political accountability.

For the Public Citizen

1. *The public citizen should strive to prevent the atrophy of
his community's own initiative and resources.*

Research has consistently pointed up the fact that the
great mass of the public is oriented toward nonparticipation
in community affairs and, unless inflamed by a controversial
issue, will tend to evince apathy, boredom, and escapism. The
future demands on the educational enterprise are so awesome
in character that they will require massive structural changes
at every governmental level. Citizens should become activists
and participants in reordering educational goals and priorities.

The traditional solutions involving distribution of scarce
resources are slowly coming under attack. Strict age-grading,
inflexible buildings, the single teacher isolated with a given
set of learners, a standard curriculum for all, are likely to be
abandoned. The public citizen should be raising hard substantive questions about the nature of his school system while
encouraging its school board and superintendent to experiment. It is well known by those in the educational fraternity
that considerable financial savings could be obtained if the
school were reorganized to use teachers more effectively.
Institutional forms are sometimes maintained after their

purpose has been replaced or are replaceable by other arrangements. Caution is required, of course, because there is no guarantee that reorganization in and of itself will provide a better product; the plan for change must have intrinsic merit and be related to a stated objective.

2. *Citizens need to insist on democratic procedures for selecting quality candidates for board membership.*

The emphasis is on quality; a procedure may be theoretically democratic but result in the election of a demagogue. Self-perpetuating mechanisms where the board selects its own membership may or may not be satisfactory; good men are likely to select good men; bad men choose similar types. The best way for the concerned citizen to monitor school board elections is to insist on a community caucus arrangement or a responsible partisan political arrangement. The office seeks the man is not a bad principle to use in selecting a public-spirited board member, even though the mechanism does make possible the cooptation of citizen action groups.

3. *Citizens should demand full documentary evidence for important school decisions.*

It is axiomatic to say that the schools belong to the people. However, citizens are notoriously ill informed about school issues and are sometimes led to vote against legitimate proposals on the basis of dishonest propaganda. The citizen's duty is to find out the facts in major controversies by reading the literature prepared by the school system, by attending board meetings and asking relevant questions, by personal observation, and by any other means at his disposal. If citizens assumed an inquiring attitude of this type, local control would never become a myth; it would become a reality. Citizen interest would neutralize power disequilibriums, would dampen the sting of veto groups who stand in the background, would negate the excesses of the news media, would strengthen board-superintendent relationships, and would be the most valuable innovation which has ever hit the educational landscape.

We recommend the investment concept of education. The most hardnosed taxpayer with no children should recognize that the return to the community on the dollar invested far exceeds any other investment he can make. It is a fact of life that a maintenance orientation is bad economics and a development orientation is at worst a low risk.

4. *Citizens are advised to be wary of ideological polarizations in the body politic.*

There is considerable danger that we are approaching a period where pluralism has become so fragmented that countless interest groups appear on nearly all educational issues as they arise. The political party suggestion might provide a framework for the aggregation of some of these interests into identifiable party programs or platforms. We are fast reaching, in many communities, the situation where there are so many interest groups and so many different leaders thrown up on every policy issue that neither the board of education nor the practicing administrators can hope to settle all the grievances indicated. In addition, there is the real danger that a vast number of competing interests may create a situation where we become so political, as has happened in many African countries, that educational policy will become even more rigid than it presently is.

APPENDIX A

RESEARCH
PROCEDURES

Studies of community structures reveal a disconcerting correlation between method and the type of community; so-called reputational methods have showed findings of dominated communities, while more statistically oriented studies, especially those oriented toward membership and leadership in organizations, have uncovered factional and pluralistic communities. That different methods frequently produce different results is well known in the behavioral sciences.

THE REPUTATIONAL METHOD

Although the reputational method used to study power varies somewhat from one researcher to another, it rests on the common assumption that men nominated as powerful can best serve as informants about who controls the decision-making process.[1]

The advantage of the method from a research standpoint is its simplicity. The first step in identifying power figures is to determine what geographical area and level of government are to be considered. The power structure in Milwaukee, Wisconsin, may or may not overlap with statewide influential persons. In our research the area is restricted to local school districts.

The second step is to determine what individuals in the area under study are most likely to have inside information as to what the social structure is all about. Likely candidates are newspaper editors, bankers, leading businessmen, local government officials, clergymen, labor figures, and other prominent people.

Once this pool of informants has been selected, it is customary to have interviewers ask who these persons think have the clout to influence decisions in a particular realm. Eventually, some individuals receive more nominations than others and hence become the prime subjects for intensive study. This method may be strengthened by concentrating on how specific issues, such as a rejection of a school bond issue, were actually affected by those perceived as powerful.

The method is particularly suited for comparative studies; a team of interviewers can enter communities for a short period of time and by intensive interviewing obtain a substantial amount of data.

The selection of respondents in case studies has many well known difficulties. Whom does one interview and how does one validate these data? The reputational method, as a technique for selecting informants, has been subjected to intense criticism. These reservations must be pointed out as conditions qualifying the findings of this study.

While the critique of the reputational method has often been vitriolic, some of the suggested limitations have a solid scientific base:

1. Heard, who interviewed more than 500 politicians in connection with V. O. Key's study of Southern politics,[2] concluded that "even responsible citizens succumb to the temptation to repeat political gossip as though it were gospel." [3] In every state the interviewer encountered questionable gossip that permeated the whole political community and was accepted by experienced observers as reliable. He made a point of tracing some of this gossip to its source. Numbers of items were found to have originated in nothing more substantial than speculation in high quarters or simply a misquotation of an informed individual.

To offset this human tendency we limited the classification of communities, boards, and superintendents to reports of power and conflict relations given by persons who were directly involved in each event they were reporting. We did listen to rumors, of course, and these helped to delineate the importance of the attitudinal frame of reference in factional and pluralistic communities.

2. The reputational method, as usually employed, elicits responses concerning influence on general rather than specific issues, and the evidence from studies in at least some communities points to the limited sphere of influence for most leaders.[4] In dominated communities, the overlap of leaders from one issue to another is somewhat greater, but still not overwhelming.[5] In either case, the use of questions as to "who around here has the most influence?" without specifying

with regard to what issue, assumes rather than tests the generality of influence. If the study is done in a community in which influence is highly specific, the generalized question of influence does not allow the researcher to discover that phenomenon.

To avoid this weakness we asked our informants to name leaders and persons of influence within the educational system, both generally and on specific educational problems, such as taxes and sex education.

3. The questions used in the reputational method usually center on potential power rather than on power that is being clearly exercised. At its best, then, the reputational method discovers persons who can serve as *informants* concerning the exercise of power, unless, of course, one is searching for power potential, a use of the method made by Hanson.[6]

We employed the reputational method to identify informants, but we accepted only those data reported by our respondents which bore directly upon their exercise of or submission to power. Further, we depended heavily upon officially elected persons responsible for decision-making, and in interviews with them we restricted ourselves to data on power exercised.

4. Closely associated with the previous point is the fact that citizens in general do not know who wields power. It is for this reason that Rose suggested the term "knowledgeables" in developing a "pool" of power actors.[7]

We defined school superintendents and school board members as "knowledgeables," and since our data relate most directly to educational issues, these "knowledgeables" would be the most likely to know whether or not power was being exercised on them.

5. Both those who use the reputational method and those who are critical of it have pointed to its ability to predict the outcome of decision-making processes, especially in elections, as a useful test of its validity. The success of those making predictions based on data of this kind has been varied.

Nor do we agree that predicting an election, or a vote on a bond issue, is a necessary or sufficient test of the reputational method. Indeed, elections represent one means by which citizens can overcome the control of power figures.

6. Our own criticism of current methodology in the study of power and conflict is that it is far less rigorous than even the comparatively poor methodology of the behavioral sciences generally. With this we are confident none of the critics or researchers in the field would disagree. But to develop more sophisticated techniques, structured questions, and statistical analyses in an area in which so little is actually known would be premature. At this point, a preferable strategy is to develop whatever understanding can be gleaned from studies using techniques bordering on the intuitive, be as honest as possible about methodology, and "take the lumps" from anticipated critics.

Indeed, one decision we made in the direction of scientific rigor was to limit ourselves to the educational sphere. Clearly the model can be tested within the framework of a single institutional order, but, logically, it also applies across the board. And this we have not tested.

This study is, therefore, extensive rather than intensive; each community is examined less intensively than the authors of previous case studies, and the study follows a parallel style to large surveys of individuals and families.

THE SELECTION OF COMMUNITIES

In our definition of community we mean both the geographical area within which the school board and superintendent have jurisdiction and the more generally socially meaningful groupings in which well-organized power structures might operate. Since the boundaries of school districts and viable communities frequently do not correspond perfectly, the selection of the unit of analysis for this study was exceedingly difficult.

We decided to ameliorate this problem by designating the school district as the basic unit of analysis and studying the largest community center in that district. As it actually worked out, the procedure had to be changed, because interviews of both board members and community power figures took us far beyond what could be considered the community boundaries of the largest center.

Actually, the model itself should have led us to predict the necessity to loosen the definition of the unit of analysis: a centralized school district, in which the schools of two communities have been integrated, may experience factionalism as a result of having two community centers. Such communities, traditionally jealous rivals, may find it extremely difficult to get together on system-wide concerns.

As in most studies, the population had to be severely limited because of the availability of funds and the uncertainty with which researchers proceed when testing their own models; therefore, it was decided to restrict the study to two regions of the United States, the Northeast and the Midwest. Communities were taken from the following states: New York, Pennsylvania, Connecticut, New Jersey, Minnesota, Wisconsin, and Illinois.

Originally the intention was to select a probability sample within the states. However, as we proceeded with our field research we discovered that we were not identifying a sufficient number of factional communities. In reflecting on this, we decided that factional communities often restore themselves to one of the other three types unless there is an important issue over which the two or three factions strongly disagree. Therefore, unless the researcher is in the community at the time a factional dispute is occurring, he runs the risk of overlooking the factional structure. Newspapers and other documents are possible sources of information on past conflicts, but these sources might present a biased picture since conflict is reported variously in different communities.

A further limitation was imposed by the nature of the model itself. Only those school districts in which the superintendent had been in his present position for at least two years were drawn in the final sample. We reasoned that school board members and community power figures would be unable to perceive accurately the leadership role of the school superintendent if he had only recently assumed office. Furthermore, a new superintendent would have meager information concerning either attempts to exert influence by community influentials or the operational patterns of relationships established by the school board.

It was agreed upon by the researchers and the sponsoring agency that approximately fifty cases would be sufficient to test the model and the relationships it predicts. We decided arbitrarily to make the final sample consist of a relatively equal number of cases in each region from each of four community types: rural, small city, suburban, and large urban.

We did not seek parameters but rather attempted to analyze relationships that would allow us to seek parameters in the future. Otherwise, the test of the model would have been impossible, given the number of cases we were able to study.

The decision to forego parameters in order to obtain adequate numbers of each community type resulted in a less than even distribution of cases in each of the stratified groupings. The final distribution resulted in sixteen school districts which were considered rural (where the community center was 2,500 or less); ten suburban communities; fourteen districts which were considered small urban (2,500 to 24,999 in the population center); and eleven districts were large urban in nature (25,000 or above).

TABLE 4

DISTRIBUTION OF TYPES OF COMMUNITY
POWER STRUCTURES

TYPE OF COMMUNITY POWER STRUCTURE	Number of Communities
Dominated	8
Factional	7
Pluralistic	23
Inert	13
TOTAL	51

The decision to let the strata become somewhat imbalanced helped considerably in providing a sufficient number of cases of each type of power structure and each type of school board, as well as each type of professional role. Thereby we minimized the risk of generalizing from completely unique cases. The distribution of the various types indicated in the model are presented in Tables 4–6.

TABLE 5

DISTRIBUTION OF TYPES OF SCHOOL
BOARD STRUCTURES

TYPE OF SCHOOL BOARD	Number of School Boards
Dominated	8
Factional	10
Status Congruent	22
Sanctioning	11
TOTAL	51

TABLE 6

DISTRIBUTION OF TYPES OF ROLES
OF SUPERINTENDENTS

TYPE OF ROLE	Number of Superintendents
Functionary	8
Political Strategist	9
Professional Adviser	21
Decision Maker	13
TOTAL	51

THE SELECTION OF LEADERS

The research design called for interviewing the superintendent, the school board members, and both formal and informal power figures in the community. The superintendent was asked to suggest the names of important people in the community with respect to school issues. Then the school board members were interviewed and they were similarly asked to nominate the names of influentials with respect to educational issues. Leaders in prominent positions such as the city manager, newspaper editor, and the like, were sought out in each community and they were also asked to suggest names. Finally, nominations were obtained from the community leaders themselves.

Two criteria were used in selecting the community power figures by the reputational method: the number of times the person's name was mentioned by the superintendent, the school board members, and other influentials and persons possibly not mentioned but strongly associated with some event or faction. A person mentioned by everyone concerned clearly would be interviewed; a person mentioned only once or twice normally would not be interviewed unless influence or power relationships were suspected.

THE INTERVIEW

Interviews were conducted according to a guide, but the interviewers were asked to pursue leads possibly indicating the presence of power relations. This succeeded to varying degrees, depending upon the interviewer, the respondent, and the setting.

Almost all interviews were recorded on tape and later transcribed. We have quoted freely from these protocols throughout the text. The interviews were used in a manner analogous to the biologist's use of a microscope. They told us about events which had occurred; they were sources of data and were given consideration commensurate with their usefulness.

Perhaps a word of caution should be offered in interpreting the above statement. A series of interviews indicating that no power relationships existed in the past and that the board largely takes the recommendations of the professional it has hired to make such recommendations, would lead to the classification of a community as inert in power structure and to a classification of a school board as sanctioning. But, in a series of twelve interviews with community leaders, three or four respondents might tell us of specific events in which the exercise of power and influence was apparent. An astute interviewer will be able to follow up in such instances to see whether such events actually occurred. One common check is the correspondence between responses given by two respondents to two different interviewers. If the occurrence of an event can be established, even though the other eight interviews in the example above report no such event, then these eight interviews are considered to be less valid than those which do report the event.

CLASSIFICATION PROCEDURES

It is clearly of paramount importance to have interviewers and judges who are as sensitive to the social situation with respect to power and influence as they are objective in their classifications of communities. Since the knowledge of the model could itself easily have a halo effect and influence people to see power where none existed, several precautions were taken.

It was decided to introduce slightly different procedures in the two geographical areas to see if different results occurred. In the Midwest classifications were made by the team, and, although minority reports were allowed, a team judgment or a group decision was made. In the Northeast there was discussion among the interviewers as to what had occurred in the community, the school board, and the like, but the classifications were the private votes of the interviewer team. This difference in procedure was expected to eliminate the influence that might be exerted by unusually articulate members of the interviewer team, though there is no reason to believe that the articulate members would be more likely to support than reject the model as fitting any given community.

The differences resulting from this variation in research methods were not surprising. As would be expected, there was somewhat more disagreement in the Northeast, where individual votes were taken, than there was in the Midwest where a group decision was arrived at after lengthy discussion. The extent of the discussions was determined by the amount of time needed to arrive at some consensus. However, the deviant votes were as often in favor of fitting the pattern of the model as they were diverging from it.

The interviewers were assured and indeed urged not to try to make data fit the patterns or even the classifications suggested by the model. In the selection of interviewers, there was an attempt to find persons who gave the appearance of being sufficiently receptive to elicit the data needed in the interview but who were sufficiently aggressive to differ with the research directors on substantive issues. The training in interviewing was given by field chiefs who themselves were independent and autonomous men. This, we hoped, would decrease the influence of the research directors and their identification with the model. All of the interviewers were graduate students who presumably had been socialized into the scientific attitude to varying degrees.

Regardless of the slight differences in method, the percentage of communities which fit or did not fit the patterns suggested by the model was equal in the two regions using the two classification techniques. The different procedures would be especially important in studies in which the relative frequencies in each type of pattern were a major problem of the research.

STATISTICAL PROCEDURES

In the exploratory research involved in the development of any relatively new area of sociology, there has been a tendency either to ignore statistical analysis completely or to force data into sophisticated procedures that give these data only the appearance of precision, elegance of design, and requisite validity and reliability. In the present study, an attempt was made to use some statistical devices but to use simpler procedures where these were applicable.

In testing the model itself, the requirement is that a nonparametric statistic be used for testing the significance of any correlation coefficient, since there was no attempt to search for parameters of the various types of communities, school boards, and roles. The selection of the test of significance was partly determined by the types of correlation coefficient that was available for an R by C table. Four types are posited in the community, four in the school board structure, and four in the role of the superintendent. These types are not ranked on a basis of any type of underlying dimension, but simply differ qualitatively with respect to the manner in which power is exercised, decisions are made, and roles played. There is, however, a pattern of frequencies that is dictated by the nature of the model which requires that, if the model is to be confirmed, there must be a heavy concentration in certain cells of the table and very little concentration of "errors" in other cells of the table.

The coefficient of contingency has been employed in

studies with similar data in the past. However, it was decided phi-coefficient would be more appropriate for use in the present study (11). Like the coefficient of contingency, the phi-coefficient employs chi-square as a test of significance and the chi-square itself is used in the computation of the phi-coefficient for R by C. The formula for phi is as follows:

$$\text{Phi}' = \sqrt{\frac{\text{chi}^2}{N} (L - 1)}$$

when L is the smaller of rows or columns. The chi-square is the usual one for four-by-four tables, in which the computation is based on the difference between expected frequencies and observed frequencies. Traditionally, in social research, tables are collapsed into fewer rows and columns when some expected frequencies are below five. However, a study by Cochran indicated that such a reduction in rows and columns was not necessary when some of the expected frequencies were above five in a more than two-by-two table.[8] The findings of the Cochran study were employed in the present analysis and, because of the importance of studying each category independently, the chi-squares were computed in spite of the fact that some expected frequencies were below five.

NOTES

1. Arnold M. Rose, *The Power Structure: Political Process in American Society,* New York: Oxford University Press, 1967.

2. V. O. Key, *Politics, Parties, and Pressure Groups,* New York: Thomas Y. Crowell, 1958.

3. Alexander Heard, "Interviewing Southern Politicians," *American Political Science Review* 44, December, 1950, p. 896.

4. Robert A. Dahl, *Who Governs?,* New Haven: Yale University Press, 1961.

5. William V. D'Antonio and Eugene Erickson, "The Reputational Technique as a Measure of Community Power: An Evaluation Based on Comparative and Longitudinal Study," *American Sociological Review* 27, June, 1962, pp. 362–376.

6. Robert C. Hanson, "Predicting a Community Decision," *American Sociological Review* 24, October, 1959, pp. 662–71.

7. Rose, *The Power Structure.*

8. William G. Cochran, "The X^2 Test of Goodness of Fit," *The Annals of Mathematical Statistics* 23, September, 1952.

APPENDIX B

LIST
OF PROBE
QUESTIONS

Following are the guideline questions used to probe the situation of power and conflict in each community. Power relations represent highly sensitive areas in some communities, and the probe questions were used merely to keep the conversation going until clues as to power and conflict were found by the interviewer. If and when such clues became apparent, the interviewer pursued the situation in a way dictated by the reported events. When clues developed into events of central interest to this research, the interviewer sometimes did not return to the list of probe questions. In reading over the transcript of interviews, we found most significant those cases in which events rather than this list of questions dictated the later part of the interview.

SUPERINTENDENT OF SCHOOLS

The purpose of this research is to learn in a systematic way about school-community relationships in this community; by studying a number of different communities, we hope to be able to establish some findings which may be beneficial to superintendents and board members. All answers to this interview schedule are absolutely confidential. Any results will be presented in anonymous or statistical form.

We would like to ask a few brief questions about yourself and your background to help us in our final analysis.

1.   How long have you been superintendent in this community?

2.   How long have you been a superintendent?

3.   Were you in this school district just before you became superintendent? If yes, what position?

4.   Sex (obvious but record it) Male   Female

5.   How old were you on your last birthday?

6.   Marital status?

7.   What is your religious affiliation? (If Protestant, probe for denomination)

We would now like to get some idea from you about the general nature of leadership and decision-making in this community. Our questions are in three general areas: the school board, the community, the role of the superintendent.

I. The School Board

A. Criteria for Selection and Orientation of Board Members

 1. Suppose a man wanted to become a Board member in this community. Could you give me your ideas about what he would have to do and the qualifications he would need? (If not clear—would he have to belong to any particular organization or clubs?)
 2. What formal procedures exist for the orientation of new members?
 3. What informal procedures exist for the orientation of new members?
 4. Do changes in membership affect Board operation much?
 5. What role, if any, do you play in the selection of new Board members?

B. Board Organization

 1. How is the chairman of the Board elected?
 2. Are there any criteria for his election (tenure of office, professional background, etc.)?

C. Controversial issues.

 1. When you have a controversial issue come up before the Board which cannot be easily resolved, how does the Board go about making a decision?
 2. What role do you play in this process?
 3. On crucial and controversial issues, does your Board usually take your advice? Whose advice does it take in addition to yours?
 4. Are crucial and controversial issues discussed ahead of time and can you usually predict the vote?

5. On these matters does the Board usually seek a unanimous vote?

6. Does debate make a difference in votes on controversial issues? What kind of a difference?

7. Are there any controversial issues which you would be reluctant to bring up before the Board in open meetings? What are they and why would you be reluctant?

8. Are there any controversial issues which you would be reluctant to bring up before the Board in closed or executive meetings? What are they and why would you be reluctant?

9. Often Boards find it desirable to discuss really knotty problems outside the Board meetings. Does your Board find it helpful to talk over school problems informally with people in the community? With whom does the Board talk?

10. Suppose a new major educational project (bond issue for new school, major curricular revision) needed to be pushed through, whom would you nominate to a committee in order to insure probability of success? Assume that the power to nominate such a committee had been delegated to you.

II. Community

A. Controversial Issues

1. All school-community relationships are characterized by some problems, great or small. What are the chief problems between the school system and the community here?

2. During the last two years, what specific knotty issues has this community experienced concerning education?

3. How were these issues resolved?

4. What was your role in resolving these issues?

B. Community Groups

1. Some studies of other communities have shown that a small group pretty well runs local affairs and makes most of the important decisions. In your opinion is this an accurate description of the way in which things are run here? Why is that?

2. Could such a situation develop in this community?

3. As you know, in every community there are organizations, informal groups, and the like which exert considerable influence, often good, sometimes bad, on community issues, including educational issues. How has the School Board been affected by such influence?

4. What groups have exerted influence?

5. What did they do to exert influence?

6. Is it the same group for different issues?

7. Have sides or factions ever developed around these issues?

8. What kind of effect have these influences had on your job as superintendent?

9. Suppose a major community project (new hospital, urban renewal, enticing new industry) needed to be pushed through, whom would you nominate to a committee in order to assure probability of success? Assume that the power to appoint such a committee has been delegated to you.

NOTE: Try to find out who these people are. Leaders of industry (Morse Chain), city official (attorney) or whatever.

III. The Role of the Superintendent

A. At Board Meetings
   1. What do you do during Board meetings?
   2. How often do you speak?
   3. Where do you sit?
   4. Do you act differently at open and closed meetings of the Board?

B. In the Community
   1. A superintendent who wishes to have good schools often needs to consult friends and community leaders outside the School Board to find out how the community feels on issues. Whom do you talk to informally about such things?
   2. Whose opinion do you value most highly?

C. Board Problems
   1. What would be the reaction of your Board of Education if you did any of the following things?
      a. If you argued vigorously against a policy which the Board strongly supported.
      b. If you make a series of decisions which you felt were for the good of the school but which were unpopular in the community.
      c. If you did not participate in local civic affairs.
   2. If you had been a Board member, what would you have done in handling _____ problems?
   3. If you had been a citizen of the community, what would have been your position on _____ problems?

COMMUNITY INFLUENTIALS

The purpose of our research is to learn in a systematic way about school-community relationships in this community; by studying a number of different communities we hope to be able to establish some findings which may be beneficial to superintendents and board members generally. All answers to this interview schedule are absolutely confidential. Any results will be presented in an anonymous or statistical form.

We would like to ask a few brief questions about yourself and your background to help us in our final analysis.

1. How long have you lived in this school community?
2. Sex (obvious but record it)   Male   Female
3. How old were you on your last birthday?
4. Marital status?
5. What was the last grade of school you completed?
6. What is your present occupation in as precise terms as possible?
7. What is your religious affiliation? (If Protestant, probe for denomination)

We would now like to get some idea from you about the general nature of leadership and decision-making in this community. Our questions are in three general areas: the school board, the community, the role of the superintendent.

I. The School Board

A. Criteria for Selection and Orientation of Board Members

   1. Suppose a man wanted to become a Board member in this community. Could you give me your ideas about what he would have to do and the qualifications he would need? (If not clear—would he have to belong to any particular organization or clubs?)
   2. In your opinion, do changes in Board membership affect board operation much?
   3. What is the role of the superintendent in the selection of new Board members?

B. Controversial Issues
   1. When a controversial issue comes up before the Board which cannot be easily resolved, how does the Board go about making a decision?
   2. On crucial and controversial issues, does the Board usually hold full discussions ahead of the decision, and can you predict the outcome on such issues ahead of time.
   3. Is there usually a unanimous vote on controversial issues?
   4. Often Boards find it desirable to discuss really knotty problems outside the Board meetings. Does your Board find it helpful to talk over school problems informally with people in the community? With whom do they talk?
   5. How would you get your point of view across to the Board of Education?
   6. Suppose a major educational project (bond issue for new school, major curricular revision) needed to be pushed through, who would you nominate to a committee in order to insure probability of success?

II. The Community

A. Problems
   1. All school-community relationships are characterized by some problems, great or small. What are the chief problems between Board and community here?
   2. During the last two years, what specific knotty issues has this community experienced concerning education?
   3. How were these issues resolved?
   4. What was the superintendent's role in resolving those issues?
   5. Did you take an active role in any of these problems?
   6. Do Board members ever seek your advice? Which ones?
   7. Is there much disagreement among citizens in general over school matters?
   8. Do people in this community discuss school matters very much?

B. Community Groups
   1. Some studies of other communities have shown that a small group pretty well runs local affairs and makes most of the important decisions. In your opinion is this an accurate description of the way things are run here? Why?
   2. Could such a situation develop in this community?
   3. As you know, in every community there are organizations, informal groups, and the like which exert considerable influence, often good, sometimes bad, on community issues, including educational issues.

How has the School Board been influenced by such groups in this community?

4. What groups have exerted influence?
5. What did they do to exert influence?
6. Is it the same group for different issues?
7. Have sides or factions ever developed around these issues?
8. Suppose a major community project (new hospital, urban renewal, enticing new industry) needed to be pushed through, who would you nominate to a committee in order to insure probability of success? (List names below)

III. The Role of the Superintendent

A. Superintendent Reaction to Problems
1. What would be your reaction if your superintendent did any of the following things:
   a. If he argued vigorously against a policy which the Board strongly supported.
   b. If he made a series of decisions which you felt were for the good of the school but which were unpopular in the community.
   c. If he did not participate in local civic affairs.
2. If you had been superintendent, how would you have handled _____ problems?
3. What kind of an educational leader do you think your superintendent is?

SCHOOL BOARD MEMBERS

The purpose of our research is to learn in a systematic way about school community relationships in this community; by studying a number of different communities, we hope to be able to establish some findings which may be beneficial to superintendents and board members. All answers to this interview schedule are absolutely confidential. Any results will be presented in an anonymous or statistical form.

We would like to ask a few brief questions about yourself and your background to help us in our final analysis.

1. How long have you lived in this school community?
2. Sex (obvious but record it) Male _____ Female _____
3. How old were you on your last birthday?
4. Marital status?
5. How long have you been a Board member?
6. What was the last grade of school you completed?
7. What is your present occupation in as precise terms as possible?
8. What is your religious affiliation? (If Protestant, probe for denomination)

We would now like to get some idea from you about the general nature of leadership and decision-making in this community. Our questions are in three general areas: the school board, the community, the role of the superintendent.

I. The School Board

A. Criteria for Selection and Orientation of Board Members

   1. Suppose a man wanted to become a Board member in this community. Could you give me your ideas about what he would have to do and the qualifications he would need? (If not clear—would he have to belong to any particular organization or clubs?)
   2. How did you tackle the job of learning to become a Board member?
   3. What formal procedures exist for the orientation of new members?
   4. What informal procedures exist for the orientation of new members?
   5. From whom did you receive the most assistance in learning the job?
   6. Do changes in membership affect board operation much?
   7. What is the role of the superintendent in the selection of new Board members? (If not covered in previous questions)

B. Board Organization

   1. How is the chairman of the Board elected?
   2. Are there any criteria for his election (tenure of office, professional background, etc.)?

C. Controversial Issues

   1. When you have a controversial issue come up before the Board which cannot be easily resolved, how does the Board go about making a decision?
   2. What role do you play in this process?
   3. On crucial and controversial issues, does your Board

usually take your advice? Whose advice does it take?

4. On crucial and controversial issues, does the Board usually discuss it ahead of time and can you predict the vote?

5. On these matters does the Board usually seek a unanimous vote?

6. Does debate make a difference in votes on controversial issues? How?

7. Are there any controversial issues which you would be reluctant to bring up before the Board in open meetings? What are they and why would you be reluctant?

8. Are there any controversial issues which you would be reluctant to bring up before the Board in closed or executive meetings? What are they and why would you be reluctant?

9. Often Boards find it desirable to discuss really knotty problems outside the Board meetings. Does the Board find it helpful to talk over school problems informally with people in the community? With whom do you talk?

10. Suppose a major educational project (bond issue for new school, major curricular revision) needed to be pushed through, who would you nominate to a committee in order to insure probability of success? Assume the power to appoint has been delegated to you. NOTE: Look for differences, if any.

II. The Community

A. Problems

1. All school-community relationships are characterized

by some problems, great or small. What are the chief problems between the Board and community here?

2. During the last two years, what specific knotty issues has this community experienced concerning education?

3. How were these issues resolved?

4. What was the superintendent's role in resolving these issues?

B. Community Groups

1. Some studies of other communities have shown that a small group pretty well runs local affairs and makes most of the important decisions. In your opinion is this an accurate description of the way things are run here? Why?

2. Could such a situation develop in this community?

3. As you know, in every community there are organizations, informal groups, and the like which exert considerable influence, often good, sometimes bad, on community issues, including educational issues. How has the School Board been affected by such influence?

4. What groups have exerted influence?

5. What did they do to exert influence?

6. Is it the same group for different issues?

7. Have sides or factions ever developed around these issues?

8. Suppose a major community project (new hospital, urban renewal, enticing new industry) needed to be pushed through, who would you nominate to a committee in order to insure probability of success? As-

sume the power to appoint has been delegated to you. (List names below).

NOTE: Try to find out who these people are. Leaders of industry (Morse Chain), city official (attorney) or whatever.

III. The Role of the Superintendent

A. Superintendent at Board Meetings
   1. What does the superintendent do during Board meetings?
   2. How often does he speak?
   3. Where does he sit?
   4. Is there any difference in his behavior between open and closed Board meetings?
B. Superintendent Reaction to Problems
   1. What would be your reaction if your superintendent did any of the following things:
      a. If he argued vigorously against a policy which the Board strongly supported.
      b. If he made a series of decisions which you felt were for the good of the school but which were unpopular in the community.
      c. If he did not participate in local civic affairs.
   2. What would you have done in handling _____ problem if you had been the superintendent?

BIBLIOGRAPHY

Agger, Robert E. "Power Attributions in the Local Community." *Social Forces* 34 (1956): 322–331.

Agger, Robert E. and Goldrich, Daniel. "Community Power Structures and Partisanship." *American Sociological Review* 23 (1958): 383–392.

Agger, Robert E., Goldrich, Daniel, and Swanson, Bert E. *The Rulers and the Ruled*. New York: John Wiley and Sons, Inc., 1964.

Agger, Robert E. and Ostrom, Vincent. "The Political Structure of a Small Community." *Public Opinion Quarterly* 20 (1956): 81–89.

Anton, Thomas J. "Power, Pluralism, and Local Politics." *Administrative Science Quarterly* 7 (1963): 425–457.

Bachrach, Peter and Baratz, Morton S. "Two Faces of Power." *American Political Science Review* 56 (1962): 947–952.

Banfield, Edward C. *Big City Politics.* New York: Random House, 1965.

Banfield, Edward C. and Wilson, James Q. *City Politics.* Cambridge, Massachusetts: Harvard University Press, 1963.

Barnard, Chester I. *The Functions of the Executive.* Cambridge, Massachusetts: Harvard University Press, 1938.

Barth, Ernest and Abu-Laban, Baha. "Power Structure and the Negro Sub-Community." *American Sociological Review* 24 (1959): 69–76.

Bell, Daniel. *The End of Ideology.* Glencoe, Illinois: The Free Press, 1962.

Bendiner, Robert. *The Politics of Schools: A Crisis in Self-Government.* New York: Harper and Row, 1969.

Bierstedt, Robert M. "An Analysis of Social Power." *American Sociological Review* 15 (1950).

Blau, Peter M. *Exchange and Power in Social Life.* New York: John Wiley and Sons, 1964.

Brogan, Denis W. "LBJ and the American Intellectuals," *Encounter* 32 (1969): 68–77.

Campbell, Alan K. "Educational Policy-Making Studied in Large Cities." *American School Board Journal* (1967): 16–24.

Campbell, Angus, Gurin, Gerald, and Miller, Warren E. *The Voter Decides.* Evanston, Illinois: Row, Peterson, 1954.

Campbell, Angus, Converse, Philip E., Miller, Warren E., and Stokes, Donald E. *Elections and The Political Order.* New York: John Wiley and Sons, 1966.

Coleman, James S. *Community Conflict.* Glencoe, Illinois: The Free Press, 1957.

Coser, Lewis A. *The Functions of Social Conflict.* Glencoe, Illinois: The Free Press, 1956.

Dahl, Robert A. "The Concept of Power." *Behavioral Science* 2 (1957): 201–215.

Dahl, Robert A. *Who Governs?* New Haven: Yale University Press, 1961.

Dahl, Robert A. *Modern Political Analysis.* Englewood Cliffs, New Jersey: Prentice-Hall, Inc., 1965.

Dahrendorf, Ralf. *Class and Class Conflict in Industrial Society.* Stanford, California: Stanford University Press, 1959.

D'Antonio, William V. and Ehrlich, Howard J., eds., *Power and Democracy in America.* Notre Dame, Indiana: University of Notre Dame Press, 1961.

D'Antonio, William V. and Erickson, Eugene C. "The Reputational Technique as a Measure of Community Power." *American Sociological Review* 27 (1962): 363–376.

D'Antonio, William V. and Form, William H. *Influentials in Two Border Cities: A Study in Community Decision-Making.* Notre Dame, Indiana: University of Notre Dame Press, 1965.

Easton, David. *The Political System, An Inquiry into the State of Political Science.* New York: Alfred A. Knopf, 1953.

Easton, David. *A Systems Analysis of Political Life.* New York: John Wiley and Sons, 1965.

Emerson, Richard M. "Power-Dependence Relations." *American Sociological Review* 27 (1962): 31–41.

Fanelli, A. Alexander. "A Typology of Community Leadership Based on Influence and Interaction Within the Leader Subsystem." *Social Forces* 34 (1956): 332–338.

Gamson, William A. "Reputation and Resources in Community Politics." *American Journal of Sociology* 72 (1966): 121–131.

Gamson, William A. *Power and Discontent.* Homewood, Illinois: Dorsey Press, 1968.

Gamson, William A. "Rancorous Conflict in Community Politics." *American Sociological Review* 31 (1966): 71–81.

Gans, Herbert J. *The Levittowners: Ways of Life and Politics in a New Suburban Community.* New York: Random House, 1967.

Goldhammer, Herbert, and Shils, Edward A. "Types of Power and Status." *The American Journal of Sociology* 45 (1939): 171–182.

Greer, Scott. *Governing the Metropolis.* New York: John Wiley and Sons, 1962.

Haer, John L. "Social Stratification in Relation to Attitude Toward Sources of Power in a Community." *Social Forces* 35 (1956): 137–142.

Halberstam, David. "The Very Expensive Education of McGeorge Bundy." *Harper's* 239 (1969): 21–41.

Hanson, Robert C. "Predicting a Community Decision: A Test of the Miller-Form Theory." *American Sociological Review* 24 (1959): 662–671.

Hawley, Amos H. "Community Power and Urban Renewal Success." *American Journal of Sociology* 68 (1963): 422–431.

Hollingshead, August B. *Elmtown's Youth.* New York: John Wiley and Sons, 1949.

Hunter, Floyd. *Community Power Structure.* Chapel Hill: University of North Carolina Press, 1953.

Iannaccone, Laurence. *Politics in Education.* New York: The Center for Applied Research in Education, Inc., 1967.

Jennings, M. Kent. *Community Influentials: The Elites of Atlanta.* New York: Free Press of Glencoe, 1964.

Key, V. O., Jr. *Politics, Parties, and Pressure Groups.* New York: Thomas Y. Crowell, 1947.

Klapp, Orrin E., and Padgett, L. Vincent. "Power Structure and Decision-Making in a Mexican Border City." *American Journal of Sociology* 65 (1960): 400–406.

Kozol, Jonathan. *Death at an Early Age.* Boston: Houghton-Mifflin, 1967.

Latham, Earl. "The Group Basis of Politics: Notes for a Theory." *American Political Science Review* 46 (1952): 376–397.

Lindblom, Charles E. *The Policy Making Process.* Englewood Cliffs, New Jersey: Prentice-Hall, 1968.

Lipham, James M., Gregg, Russell T., and Rossmiller, Richard A. "The School Board: Resolver of Conflict?" *Administrator's Notebook* 17 (1969): 1–4.

Lowi, Theodore J. *The End of Liberation.* New York: W. W. Norton, 1969.

Lynd, Robert, and Lynd, Helen M. *Middletown in Transition.* New York: Harcourt, Brace and Co., 1937.

Malone, Joseph F. "The Lonesome Train in Levittown." *The Inter-University Case Program, Revised Edition.* Tuscaloosa, Alabama: University of Alabama Press, 1958.

Martindale, Don. *Institutions, Organizations, and Mass Society.* Boston: Houghton Mifflin Company, 1966.

Masotti, Louis H. *Education and Politics in Suburbia: The New*

Trier Experience. Cleveland: The Press of Western Reserve University. 1967.

McCarty, Donald J. "Motives for Seeking School Board Membership." (Unpublished Ph.D. dissertation, Department of Education, University of Chicago, 1959).

McCarty, Donald J. and Ramsey, Charles E. "Community Power, School Board Structure, and the Role of the Chief School Administrator." *Educational Administration Quarterly* (1968): 19–33.

Miller, Delbert C. "Decision-Making Cliques in Community Power Structures: A Comparative Study of an American and an English City." *American Journal of Sociology* 64 (1958): 299–310.

Mills, Warner E., Jr. and Davis, Harry R. *Small City Government: Seven Cases in Decision Making.* New York: Random House, 1962.

Mills, C. Wright. *The Power Elite.* New York: Oxford University Press, 1956.

Minar, David W. "The Community Basis of Conflict in School System Politics." *American Sociological Review* 31 (1966): 822–835.

Neumann, Franz L. "Approaches to the Study of Political Power." *Political Science Quarterly* 65 (1950): 161–180.

Palumbo, Dennis J. "Power and Role Specificity in Organization Theory." *Public Administration Review* 29 (1969): 237–248.

Perkins, James A. *The University in Transition.* Princeton: Princeton University Press, 1966.

Pois, Joseph. *The School Board Crisis: A Chicago Case Study.* Chicago: Educational Methods, 1964.

Polsby, Nelson W. *Community Power and Political Theory.* New Haven: Yale University Press, 1963.

Presthus, Robert V. *Men at the Top: A Study in Community Power.* New York: Oxford University Press, 1964.

Rose, Arnold. *The Power Structure: Political Process in American Society.* New York: Oxford University Press, 1967.

Sacks, Seymour, "Central City and Suburban Public Education; Fiscal Resources and Fiscal Realities," Robert J. Hanghurst, ed., *1968 NSSE Yearbook: Educational Metropolitanism.* National Society for the Study of Education, Chicago, 1968.

Sanders, Irwin T., and Ensminger, Douglas. "Alabama Rural Communities: A Study of Chilton County." *Alabama College Bulletin* 136 (1940).

Schelling, Thomas C. *The Strategy of Conflict.* Cambridge, Massachusetts: Harvard University Press, 1960.

Schermerhorn, Richard A. *Society and Power.* New York: Random House, 1964.

Schulze, Robert O. and Blumberg, Leonard U. "The Determination of Local Power Elites." *American Journal of Sociology* 63 (1957): 290–296.

Schulze, Robert O. "The Bifurcation of Power in a Satellite City," in Janowitz, Morris, ed. *Community Political Systems.* Glencoe, Illinois: The Free Press, 1961.

Seeley, John R., Sim, R. Alexander, and Loosely, Elizabeth W. *Crestwood Heights: A Study of the Culture of Suburban Life.* New York: John Wiley and Sons, Inc., 1956.

Truman, David B. *The Governmental Process: Political Interests and Public Opinion.* New York: Alfred A. Knopf, 1951.

Tucker, Robert C. "The Theory of Charismatic Leadership." *Daedalus* 7 (1968): 731–756.

Vidich, Arthur J. and Bensman, Joseph. *Smalltown in Mass Society: Class, Power, and Religion in a Rural Community.* Princeton: Princeton University Press, 1958.

Weber, Max. *From Max Weber: Essays in Sociology.* Gerth, H. H. and Mills, C. W., eds. New York: Oxford University Press, 1946.

Weber, Max. *The Theory of Social and Economic Organization.* New York: Oxford University Press, 1947.

Williams, Oliver P. "A Typology for Comparative Local Government." *Midwest Journal of Political Science* 5 (1961): 150–165.

Williams, Robin M., Jr. *American Society: A Sociological Interpretation.* New York: Alfred A. Knopf, 1961.

Wolfinger, Raymond E. "Reputation and Reality in the Study of 'Community Power.'" *American Sociological Review* 25 (1960): 636–644.

INDEX

Subject Index

Public opinion, 145, 214, 216
Public relations, 155
Referendum, 36, 42, 205
Religion: and power, 38, 66; and voting, 110; and conflict, 29, 80–1, 86, 87, 88, 89–90, 94, 117; and pluralism, 129–30
Report card: as issue in factional community, 83–4; in pluralistic community, 129–30
Reputational method, 237–41, 246, 247, 248, 258–67
Sample of communities: size, 242, 243–5; selections, 242–5, 246; unit of analysis, 242; distribution by area, 243; distribution by size of community, 243–4
Self-fulfilling prophecy: and conflict, 89
Sex education, 48, 173, 174, 216
Sputnik and schools, 133
State aid, 154
State Education Association, 175
Student unrest, 106, 153, 177, 211–2
Superintendent: role of, 214–9; in dominated community, 20–1, 25, 29, 58, 60, 61–2, 72; in factional community, 21, 61, 77, 87–8, 103–7, 112–6, 118–9; in pluralistic community, 21, 126, 131–2, 145–50, 152, 153, 215; in inert community, 21–2, 34–5, 161, 165, 171–2, 172–5, 178–93; recommendations to, 220–9; training of, 217; forces on, 179–80; dismissal of, 30, 32–3, 64, 68, 71, 122, 104–5, 114, 115, 205
Taxes, school: in dominated community, 34, 46; in factional community, 81, 97; in pluralistic community, 144, 154; in inert community, 119, 210–1
Teachers: as board members, 55; treatment of, 102; and conflict, 119, 212–3; and parents, 173; and power, 115; recruitment of, 73–4, 119, 151, 186–7, 173; dismissal of, 70, 71, 212–3; organizations, 175, 176, 177, 212–3, 217; salaries, 175–7, 212–3; tenure, 213
Teachers' problems: in dominated community, 55, 70–1, 73–4; in factional community, 102, 119; in pluralistic community, 151; in inert community, 173, 175, 176, 177, 186–7
Vocational courses, 173
Voting: as barrier to power, 36, 42, 205
Women: and pluralism, 205